Charles Northend

The Young Declaimer

A Collection of Pieces in Poetry, Prose and Dialogue

Charles Northend

The Young Declaimer
A Collection of Pieces in Poetry, Prose and Dialogue

ISBN/EAN: 9783337372224

Printed in Europe, USA, Canada, Australia, Japan

Cover: Foto ©Thomas Meinert / pixelio.de

More available books at **www.hansebooks.com**

THE

YOUNG DECLAIMER:

BEING A COLLECTION OF PIECES IN

POETRY, PROSE, AND DIALOGUE,

DESIGNED FOR THE USE OF

PUPILS IN INTERMEDIATE SCHOOLS.

By CHARLES NORTHEND, A. M.,

AUTHOR OF "TEACHER'S ASSISTANT," "NATIONAL ORATOR,"
"CHILD'S SPEAKER," ETC.

———◆———

NEW YORK:
A. S. BARNES & CO.
1872.

CONTENTS.

PART I.—POETRY.

PART II.—PROSE.

PART III.—DIALOGUES.

PART IV.—FOR CONCERT RECITATION.

If We Would.

If we would but check the speaker
    When he spoils a neighbor's fame;
If we would but help the erring
    Ere we utter words of blame;
If we would, how many might we
    Turn from paths of sin and shame.

Ah! the wrongs that might be righted
    If we would but see the way!
Ah! the pains that might be lightened
    Every hour and every day,
If we would but hear the pleadings
    Of the hearts that go astray.

Let us step outside the stronghold
    Of our selfishness and pride;
Let us lift our fainting brothers;
    Let us strengthen ere we chide;
Let us, ere we blame the fallen,
    Hold a light to cheer and guide.

Ah, how blessed—ah, how blessed
  Earth would be if we'd but try
Thus to aid and right the weaker,
    Thus to check each brother's sigh;
Thus to walk in duty's pathway
  To our better life on high.

In each life, however lowly,
    There are seeds of mighty good;
Still, we shrink from souls appealing,
    With a timid "If we could;"
But God, who knoweth all things,
    Knows the truth is, "If we would."

Speak no Ill.

Nay, speak no ill; a kindly word
  Can never leave a sting behind;—
And oh! to breathe each tale we've heard
  Is far beneath a noble mind.
For oft a better seed is sown
  By choosing thus a kinder plan;
For if but little good we know,
  Let's speak of all the good we can.

Give me the heart that fain would hide—
  Would fain another's fault efface.
How can it please our human pride
  To prove humanity but base?

No, let it reach a higher mode—
A nobler estimate of man :
Be earnest in the search of good,
And speak of all the good we can.

Then speak no ill, but lenient be
To others' failings as your own.
If you're the first a fault to see,
Be not the first to make it known.
For life is but a passing day ;
No lips can tell how brief the stay.
Be earnest in the search for good,
And speak of all the good we may.

The World as it Is.

' The world is not so bad a world
As some would like to make it ;
Though whether good or whether bad,
Depends on how we take it.
For if we scold and fret all day,
From dewy morn till even,
This world will ne'er afford to man
A foretaste here of heaven.

This world in truth's as good a world
As e'er was known to any,
Who have not seen another yet,
And these are very many ;

And if the men, and women too,
    Have plenty of employment,
Those surely must be hard to please
    Who cannot find enjoyment.

This world is quite a clever world,
    In rain or pleasant weather,
If people would but learn to live
    In harmony together;
Nor seek to burst the kindly bond
    By love and peace cemented,
And learn that best of lessons yet,
    Always to be contented.

Then were the world a pleasant world,
    And pleasant folks were in it,
The day would pass most pleasantly
    To those who thus begin it;
And all the nameless grievances
    Brought on by borrowed troubles,
Would prove, as certainly they are,
    A mass of empty bubbles!

A Hero.

Perhaps you think a hero
    A man of giant might,
A warrior in armor,
    A champion for the right,

Who through the world goes boasting
  That wrong shall be no more;
The glory of whose exploits
  Is sung from shore to shore.

In olden times a hero
  Was such a man, I know; '
He went to battle aided
  By javelin and bow.
You all have heard of Ajax,
  Of Priam's valiant son,
And of the great Achilles,
  Who many battles won.

But now to be a hero,
  Is quite another thing;
And he who earns the title
  Is nobler than a king.
'Tis he who follows duty,
  Who scorns to be untrue;
Who's guided by his conscience,
  Not by what others do.

And you may be a hero,
  By doing all you can
To free the world from error,
  And aid your brother man.
And though no blast of trumpet
  Your greatness may proclaim,
With heartfelt benedictions
  Mankind will breathe your name.

Upward and Onward.

Battling in the cause of truth
With the zeal and strength of youth;
Upward, raise your banner higher,
Onward, urge your phalanx nigher
    To the center of the strife:
Strike, where virtue finds a foe—
Strike, while love directs the blow—
    Where the foes of man are rife.

Be your watchword truth and love,
Be your stay the strength above;
'Mid the pure, remain the purest,
'Mid the faithful, be the surest—
    Temperance your banner star.
Ask not rest, nor pray for peace,
'Till the demon foe shall cease
    Life and all its joys to mar.

Warriors in the cause of right,
Earnest in your zeal and might,
Joying in your high endeavor,
Onward press, and falter never,
    'Till the victory be won.
Shout, until the field ye gain,
Press to those which still remain,
    Battling till the work be done.
        —*Wm. Andrew Sigourney.*

The Vanity of this World.

A rosy child went forth to play,
In the first flush of hope and pride,
Where sands in silver beauty lay,
Made smooth by the retreating tide;
And, kneeling on the trackless waste,
Whence ebbed the waters many a mile,
He raised, in hot and trembling haste,
Arch, wall, and tower—a goodly pile.

But when the shades of evening fell,
Veiling the blue and peaceful deep,
The tolling of the distant bell
Called the boy builder home to sleep;
He passed a long and restless night,
Dreaming of structures tall and fair;—
He came with the returning light,
And lo, the faithless sands were bare.

Less wise than that unthinking child
Are all that breathe of mortal birth,
Who grasp, with strivings warm and wild,
The false and fading toys of ea·th.
Gold, learning, glory—what are they
Without the faith that looks on high?
The sand forts of a child at play,
Which are not when the waves go by.

Up and Doing.

Boys, be up and doing,
  For the day's begun ;
Soon will come the noontide,
  Then the set of sun ;
At your task toil bravely
  Till your work is done.

Let your hands be busy
  In some useful way ;
Don't neglect your study,
  Don't forget your play ;
For each there's time enough
  Every blessed day.

You will soon be men, boys ;
  Soon will have to take
The places of your fathers ;
  Fill it for their sake ;
And in all that's noble
  Pray be wide awake !

Boys, be kind and friendly ;
  Lend a helping hand
To the weak and feeble,
  Till alone they stand ;
And in loving others
  Fulfill God's command.

Don't be mean and selfish;
Stoop not to deceit;
In all things be manly,
Life will then be sweet,
And Death's coming find you
With your work complete.
—*Kate Cameron.*

The Poor and the Rich.

The rich man's son inherits lands,
And piles of brick and stone and gold,
And tender flesh that fears the cold,
Nor dares to wear a garment old;
A heritage, it seems to me,
One would not care to hold in fee.

The rich man's son inherits cares:
The bank may break, the factory burn,
Some breath may burst his bubble shares,
And soft white hands would scarcely earn
A living that would suit his turn;
A heritage, it seems to me,
One would not care to hold in fee.

What does the poor man's son inherit?
Stout muscles and a sinewy heart,
A hardy frame, a hardier spirit;

King of two hands, he does his part
In every useful toil and art;
A heritage, it seems to me,
A king might wish to hold in fee.

What does the poor man's son inherit?
Wishes o'erjoyed with humble things,
A rank adjudged by toil-worn merit,
Content that from enjoyment springs,
A heart that in his labor sings ;
A heritage, it seems to me,
A king might wish to hold in fee.

What does the poor man's son inherit?
A patience learned by being poor,
Courage, if sorrow come, to bear it ;
A fellow-feeling that is sure
To make the outcast bless his door ;
A heritage, it seems to me,
A king might wish to hold in fee.

Oh, rich man's son, there is a toil
That with all others level stands ;
Large charity doth never soil,
But only whitens, soft white hands;
This is the best crop from thy lands ;
A heritage, it seems to me,
Worth being rich to hold in fee.

Oh, poor man's son, scorn not thy state!
There is worse weariness than thine,—
In being merely rich and great;
Work only makes the soul to shine,
And makes rest fragrant and benign,
A heritage, it seems to me,
Worth being poor to hold in fee.

Both heirs to some six feet of sod,
Are equal in the earth at last—
Both children of the same dear God,
Prove title to your heirship vast,
By record of a well-filled past!
A heritage, it seems to me,
Well worth a life to hold in fee.

Christ in the Tempest.

All night long the winds were raging
    O'er the lake of Galilee;
All the night a little vessel
    Tossed upon the stormy sea,

And the rowers, worn with watching,
    Pressed with toil, o'erwhelmed with fear,
Toward the morning watch, a whisper
    O'er the waters, seemed to hear.

And a form amid the billows,
　Spirit-like yet firm, did tread;
And again the voice rose sweeter
　" It is I, be not afraid."

It was Jesus, and the tumult
　At His voice of peace was stilled,
While the hearts of the disciples—
　All with grateful love were filled.

Storms arise on every pathway;
　Every life the tempest knows;
Grief and pain and fearful watching
　Keep the spirit from repose.

Yet we need not walk in terror,
　Though the thunders fill the sky;
For the voice of Jesus crieth
　Through the darkness—" It is I."
　　　　　—*Eleanor S. Deane.*

An Old Maxim.

" Do as they do in Spain,
When it rains, let it rain."

The year is not all summer hours,
　And as the time goes by
The harvest and the brightest flowers
　Will hang their heads and die.

The winds of the warm bright weather
  Will roughen and chill you through,
And the clouds will gather and gather,
  And shut out all the blue.
Then "do as they do in Spain,
And if it rains, let it rain!"

All days cannot be holidays,
  For the living must be fed,
And the men must work and the women work
  To get the children bread.
And when your time is come, why then
  Your playthings put away,
And take the place of women and men
  Who work for you to-day.
Ah! "do as they do in Spain,
And if it rains, let it rain."

The world's not all a pleasure-ground,
  'Tis full of pain and ill,
And when it turns itself around,
  As turn itself it will,
And that before 'tis very long,
  Why, then, my girl and boy,
Just keep your hearts as brave and strong
  As in the time of joy,
And "do as they do in Spain,
And if it rains, let it rain!"
                              —*Alice Carey.*

Cleon and I.

Cleon hath a million acres—
    Ne'er a one have I;
Cleon dwelleth in a palace—
    In a cottage, I;
Cleon hath a dozen fortunes—
    Not a penny, I;
But the poorer of the twain is
    Cleon, and not I.

Cleon, true, possesseth acres,
    But the landscape, I;
Half the charms to me it yieldeth
    Money cannot buy;
Cleon harbors sloth and dullness,
    Freshening vigor, I;
He in velvet, I in fustian,—
    Richer man am I.

Cleon is a slave to grandeur—
    Free as thought am I;
Cleon fees a score of doctors—
    Need of none have I;
Wealth surrounded, care-environed.
    Cleon fears to die;
Death may come, he'll find me ready,
    Happier man am I.

Cleon sees no charms in Nature—
  In a daisy, I ;
Cleon hears no anthem ringing
  In the sea and sky ;
Nature sings to me forever—
  Earnest listener, I ;
State for state, with all attendants,
  Who would change ?—Not I.
                    —*Chas. Mackay.*

———◆◆◆———

The Great King and the Little King.

One day the birds all met in a tree,
  But they didn't meet to sing—
They met to argue politics
  And to choose themselves a king.
There were so many overhead,
  Coming and going back,
And so many round about the tree,
  That the air was fairly black.

Some chirped. some cried, some screamed aloud,
  Some sat with slanting eye,
For there were many candidates,
  And party strife ran high.

At last it was agreed by all
  To choose the bird whose wing
Could soar the nearest to the sky,
  And crown him for their king.

The swallow tried her strength, and then
  The blackbird and the blue,
And then the sturdy honest quail;
  But none of them would do.
Then all at once the eagle swooped
  From out the fluttering crowd,
And in a minute more his head
  Was level with a cloud.

Then what was the astonishment
  Of all the birds to see
A little wren upon his tail,
  Who cried out, "Look at me!"
So half the birds began to cry,
  And half began to sing,
For some reviled him for a knave,
  And some would have him king.

Just then an owl, who lived hard by,
  Within a hollow stub,
Called, "Wren, come down and get your crown,
  Or lose it—there's the rub!"
"Good eagle, help me," cried the wren,
  Ashamed and out of breath—
"I cannot fly so near the sky,
  And if I fall 'tis death!"

No honor such a flight as this
  To any bird could bring,
And so they named him *Regulus,*
  Which means a *little king.*
The eagle's strength was in himself,
  To fly or up or down,
And so they named him king of birds,
  And so he won his crown.

—*Alice Carey.*

"Mother's Fool."

" 'Tis plain to me," said the farmer's wife,
" Those boys will make their marks in life;
They never were made to handle a hoe,
And at once to college they ought to go;
Yes, John and Henry—'tis clear to me—
Great men in this world are sure to be ;
But Tom, he's little above a fool—
So John and Henry must go to school."

" Now, really, wife," quoth farmer Brown,
As he set his mug of cider down ;
" Tom does more work in a day, for me,
Than both of his brothers do in three.
Book learnin' will never plant beans or corn,
Nor hoe potatoes—sure as you're born ;
Nor mend a rood of broken fence ;—
For my part give me common sense."

But his wife the roost was bound to rule,
And so "the boys" were sent to school;
While Tom, of course, was left behind,
For his mother said he had no mind.

Five years at school the students spent,
Then each one into business went;
John learned to play the flute and fiddle,
And parted his hair (of course) in the middle.
Though his brother looked rather higher than he,
And hung out his shingle—"H. Brown, M. D."
Meanwhile, at home, their brother Tom,
Had taken a "notion" into his head;
Though he said not a word, but trimmed his trees,
And hoed his corn and sowed his peas;
But somehow, either "by hook or crook,"
He managed to read full many a book.

Well, the war broke out; and "Captain Tom,"
To battle a hundred soldiers led;
And when the rebel flag went down
Came marching home as "*General* Brown."
But he went to work on the farm again,
Planted his corn and sowed his grain,
Repaired the house and broken fence,
And people said he had "common sense."

Now, common sense was rather rare,
And the State House needed a portion there;

So our "family dunce " moved into town,
And people called him " Governor Brown ; "
And his brothers, that went to the city school,
Came home to live with mother's fool.

Our Garret.

Oh, I love our dim old garret,
  Love to hear its echoes call,
From the lonely nooks and corners
  Where the shadows darkly fall.

There 'tis joyous to see the sunbeams
  Through the dusty windows pour,
Lighting up the tall old rafters,
  Falling brightly on the floor.

Many hours I've spent up garret,
  Reading tales and legends old,
That I found in chests and boxes
  Filled with treasures all untold,—

Treasures of old-fashioned clothing,
  That were worn long years ago ;
Papers, books, and faded pictures
  Of the times of long ago.

Often have I watched the spiders
  Spin their web along the beam,
Little thinking that I also
  Spun the thread of life's short dream ;—

Little thinking that the shadows,
  And the sunshine on the floor,
Might be likened to the sorrows
  And the joys for me in store.

It is well for us the future
  God hath hidden from our view ,
Let us trust Him, let us love Him—
  God is wise, and good, and true

And I like to sit and listen
  To the music of the rain,
As it falls upon the shingles,
  As it patters on the pane

Oh, I love our dim old garret,
  And the memories long will last
Of the pleasant hours I've spent there,
  In the years that now are past.

—H. Rose Bond.

The Better for it.

If men cared less for wealth and fame,
   And less for battle-fields and glory ;
If writ in human hearts, a name
   Seemed better than in song and story;
If men, instead of nursing pride,
   Would learn to hate it and abhor it,—
       If more relied
       On love to guide,
The world would be the better for it.

If men dealt less in stocks and lands,
   And more in bonds and deeds fraternal,
If Love's work had more willing hands,
   To link this world to the supernal ;
If men stored up Love's oil and wine,
   In bruised human hearts to pour it ;
       If " yours " and " mine,"
       Would once combine,
The world would be the better for it.

If men would act the part of Life,
   And fewer spoil it in rehearsal;
If bigotry would sheath its knife
   Till God became more universal ;
If custom, gray with ages grown,
   Had fewer blind men to adore it,—

If talent shone
In truth alone,
The world would be the better for it.

If men were wise in little things,—
Affecting less in all their dealings:
If hearts had fewer rusted strings
To isolate their kindly feelings;
If men, when Wrong beats down the Right,
Would strike together and restore it,—
If Right made Might
In every fight,
The world would be the better for it.

—*Merry's Museum.*

A Child's Joy.

What joy it is, from day to day,
To skip and sing, and dance and play
To breathe the air, to feel the sun
And o'er the spangled meadows run.

What joy to move my limbs about,
To whoop and hallo, call and shout
Among the woods and feel as free
As any bird upon a tree.

What joy, when hungry, 'tis to eat,
What pleasure is our daily meat;
How sweet, when sleep the eyelids close,
To sink in calm and soft repose.

What joy as morn begins to break,
Refreshed and vigorous to wake—
To feel, amid the dews and flowers,
New life bestowed on all my powers.

But who bestows this constant joy
On every little girl and boy?
'Tis God, our Father, bright and wise,
Whose goodness every joy supplies.

Then let us love and praise the Lord,
And strive to know his holy word;
To do no wrong, and think no ill,
And evermore perform His will.

———◆———

The Pilot.

The curling waves with awful roar
    A little boat assailed,
And pallid fear's distracting power
    O'er all on board prevailed,—

Save one, the Captain's darling child,
    Who steadfast viewed the storm,
And, fearless, with composure smiled
    At danger's threatening form.

"And fear'st thou not?" a seaman cried,
    "While terrors overwhelm?"
"Why should I fear?" the child replied,
    "My father's at the helm."

Thus when our earthly hopes are reft,
    Our earthly comforts gone,
We still have one sure anchor left,—
    God helps, and He alone.

He to our cries will lend an ear;
    He'll give our pangs relief,—
He'll turn to smiles each twinkling tear,—
    To joy each torturing grief.

Turn, turn to Him, 'mid sorrows wild,
    When terrors overwhelm,
Remembering, like the tearless child,
    Our Father's at the helm.

My First Whistle.

Of all the toys I e'er have known,
  I loved that whistle best;
It was my first, it was my own,
And I was doubly blest.

'Twas Saturday, and afternoon,
  That school-boys' jubilee,
When the young heart is all in tune
  From book and ferule free.

I then was in my seventh year;
  The birds were all a singing;
Above a brook that rippled clear,
  A willow tree was swinging.

My brother Ben was very 'cute;
  He climbed that willow tree;
He cut a branch, and I was mute,
  The while, with ecstacy.

With pen-knife he did cut it 'round,
  And gave the bark a wring;
He shaped the mouth, and tried the sound,—
  It was a glorious thing!

I blew that whistle, full of joy—
  It echoed o'er the ground;
And never, since that simple toy,
  Such music have I found.

I've seen blue eyes and tasted wines—
  With many toys been blest,
But backward memory still inclines
  To love that whistle best.

                    —*Saunders.*

Signs of the Weather.

The hollow winds begin to blow,
The clouds look black, the glass is low;
The soot falls down, the spaniels sleep
And spiders from their cob-webs peep.
Last night the sun went pale to bed,
The moon in halos hid her head;
Hark! how the chairs and tables crack!
Old Betty's joints are on the rack:
Her corns with shooting pains torment her,
And to her bed untimely send her;
Loud quack the ducks, the sea-fowl cry,
The distant hills are looking nigh.
How restless are the snorting swine!
The busy flies disturb the kine;
Low on the grass, the swallow wings;
The cricket too how sharp she sings!
Puss, on the hearth, with velvet paws
Sits wiping o'er her whiskered jaws;
The smoke from chimneys right ascends,
Then spreading back to earth it bends;

Through the clear stream the fishes rise
And nimbly catch the incautious flies.
The glow-worms, num'rous, clear and bright,
Illumined the dewy hill last night!
At dusk the squalid toad was seen
Like quadruped stalk o'er the green.
The whirling wind the dust obeys,
And in the rapid eddy plays,
The frog has changed his yellow vest,
And in a russet coat is dressed.
Behold the rooks, how odd their flight!
They imitate the gliding kite;
In fiery red the Sun doth rise,
She wades through clouds to mount the skies.
'Twill surely rain, we see with sorrow;
No working in the fields to-morrow!

—Jennett.

It Snows.

It snows! it snows! from out the sky
The feathered flakes, how fast they fly,
Like little birds, that don't know why
They're on the chase from place to place,
While neither can the other trace.
It snows! it snows! a merry play
Is o'er us on this heavy day.

As dancers in an airy hall,
That hasn't room enough to hold them all,
While some keep up and others fall,
The atoms shift, then, thick and swift,
They drive along to form the drift
That weaving up so dazzling white,
Is rising like a wall of light.

But now the wind comes whistling loud,
To snatch and waft it as a cloud;
Or giant phantom in a shroud;
It spreads! it curls! it mounts and whirls,
At length, a mighty wing unfurls;
And then, away! but where none knows,
Or ever will.   It snows! it snows!

To-morrow will the storm be done
Then out will come the golden sun,
And we shall see, upon the run
Before his beams, in sparkling streams,
What now a curtain o'er him seems.
And thus, with life, it ever goes;
'Tis shade and shine!   It snows! it snows!

                  —*Hannah F. Gould,*

"What are the Wild Waves Saying?"

"What are the wild waves saying,
      Sailor, to thee?"
"Oh, their voice is like sweetest music
      Singing to me.
Now it swells to the roar of tempest
  Making my heart grow strong,
Now, amid its soft low murmurs
  I hear the mermaid's song."

"What are the wild waves saying
      Merchant, to thee?"
"Oh, they speak of my goodly vessels
      Far o'er the sea.
Sometimes they mock me with laughter
  When I sigh o'er my sunken gold;
Sometimes they bring me good tidings
  From the shores whence their waters rolled."

"What are the wild waves saying
      Child of fashion, to thee?"
"Oh, I heed not their ceaseless dashing,
      They never speak to me.
Or if they could, they would tell me
  Naught that I care to hear,
For sometimes their sound at midnight
  Fills me with strongest fear."

"What are the wild waves saying
    Poet, to thee?"
"One word they speak to me ever,
    ETERNITY.
Yet, all of their strange sweet music
  I may not understand
Till I read life's wondrous secret,
    Afar in the heavenly land."
              —*H. Frances Osborne.*

They Say.

"They say"—Ah! well, suppose they do,
But can they prove the story true?
Suspicion may arise from naught
But malice, envy, want of thought;
Why count yourself among the "they"
Who whisper what they dare not say?

"They say"—but why the tale rehearse,
And help to make the matter worse?
No good can possibly accrue
From telling what may be untrue;
And is it not a nobler plan
To speak of all the best you can?

"They say "—Well, if it should be so,
Why need you tell the tale of woe?
Will it the bitter wrong redress,
Or make one pang of sorrow less?
Will it the erring one restore,
Henceforth to go and sin no more?

"They say "—Oh ! pause and look within—
See how thine heart inclines to sin ;
Watch, lest in dark temptation's hour,
Thou, too, shouldst sink beneath its power.
Pity the frail, weep o'er the fall,
But speak of good, or not at all.

The Youthful Advocate.

I am but a little teetotal man,
And cannot do much, but I do what I can
    To promote the temperance cause.
I never drink ale, or any such thing
As brandy or rum, wine, whisky, or sling—
    Man's curse, and the cause of his woes.

I drink cold water, so clear and so sweet :
It quenches my thirst, gives health to my cheek,
    And brings neither sorrows nor woes.
It comes from above, so bright and so free ;
In dewdrops, it shines like pearls from the sea ;
    And in streams of abundance it flows.

Enriching the soil, it supplies us with bread,
Gives life to the flowers in the green, grassy mead,
   And meets us where'er we may rove.
The beautiful birds, in the midst of their song,
Stop and drink from the brook, as it murmurs along
   Through brake and through woodland
   and grove.

Would you sing, like the birds, with sweetness and
  power,
Or, blooming in beauty, outrival the flower,
   With cheeks fresh and healthy as mine ?
Make water your drink, and unite heart and hand
To rescue and save every child in the land,
   And the pledge of true temperance sign.

Boil it Down.

Whatever you have to say, my friend,
  Whether witty, or grave, or gay,
Condense as much as ever you can,
  And say in the readiest way ;
And whether you write of rural affairs,
  Or particular things in town,
Just take a word of friendly advice—
    Boil it down.

For if you go spluttering over a page
    When a couple of lines would do,
Your butter is spread so much, you see,
    That the bread looks plainly through ;
So when you have a story to tell,
    And would like a little renown,
To make quite sure of your wish, my friend,
                  Boil it down.

When writing an article for the press,
    Whether prose or verse, just try
To utter your thoughts in the fewest words,
    And let them be crisp and dry ;
And when it is finished, and you suppose
    It is done exactly brown,
Just look it over again, and then
                  Boil it down.

For editors do not like to print
    An article lazily long,
And the busy reader does not care
    For a couple of yards of song;
So gather your wits in the smallest space,
    If you'd win the author's crown,
And every time you write, my friend,
                  Boil it down.

"Too Deep for That."

"Yes," said Farmer Brown,
Bringing his hard fist down
    On the old oak table,—
"They say that men can talk
From Paris to New York,
    Through a sunken cable!

"'Tis perfectly absurd,
For to hear a single word,
    No man is able;
And it's clear enough to me
That this wide-spread mystery
    Is a foolish fable.

"The news we get from Rome
Is all made up at home,
    'Tis my conviction;
And that, you see, will account
For the terrible amount
    Of contradiction.

"Yes," said Farmer Brown,
Bringing his hard fist down
    On the old oak table,—
"My wife and I have tried
The experiment; we tied
    A good stout bit of cable

To the fence, just over there,
And the rocker of this chair;
   And we couldn't do it,
Though we screamed ourselves as hoarse
As tree-toads; but of course
   Not one word went through it!

"Don't talk to me, I pray,
Of fresh news every day,
   Through sunken cables:
Sea-yarns are always tough,
And I have heard enough
   Of such old fables!"

               —*Hearth and Home.*

The Robin's Rehearsal.

Out for a morning rehearsal,
   Robin, and Squirrel, and bee;
They have an orchestral meeting,
   Up in that sycamore tree.
Robin has plumes on her bonnet,
   Squirrel is dressed in his furs—
Bee wears a black and gold velvet,
   Finest of laces are hers.

"Now for our practice," said Robin,
   "You can sing *air*, Mistress Bee,

You take the *base*, Mr. Squirrel,
   That will leave *alto* for me."
Up rose their voices together,
   Squirrel song, bee song, and bird;
It was the funniest medley
   You in your life ever heard.

But among happiest singers
   Sometimes dissension will come—
"Stop, Mistress Bee," cried the squirrel,
   "You can do nothing but hum."
"Pray, what can *you* do but chatter?"
   Madam retorted, and though
She to her *friends* is all sweetness,
   She is a dangerous *foe.*

Fiercely the quarrel was raging,
   Robin said, "Here let it end;
Neither shall sing at my concert,
   Neither one now is my friend."
So in disgrace they were banished;
   Soon other birds came, and they,
Being invited by Robin,
   Joined in a sweet matinee.

Little ones, here is a lesson,
   Whether at work or at play,
Studying, talking, or singing,
   Never to anger give way.
Whoso controlleth his spirit

Greater than monarch is he;
Better than conquering chieftain,
Richer his guerdon shall be.

———————•◆•———————

"Name Unknown."

In a southern land,—by the river side,
Where the crystal waters gently glide, —
In a sunken grave, with thick grass o'ergrown,
Sleeps " A federal soldier—name unknown."

There's a narrow slab at the soldier's head,
Which the rain has washed with its pearly thread,
Till we scarce can read, on the head-board lone,
This: " A fed ral soldier—name unknown,"

He had fought all day, ere he bravely fell,
'Neath the dear old flag that he loved so well,
Till the stars of eve in sweet pity shone
On " A federal soldier—name unknown."

Then a stranger had scooped a shallow grave,
'Neath the dreamy light which the moonbeams gave;
And laid him down—with a board for a stone,
Marked—" A federal soldier—name unknown."

There are anxious hearts in a northern home
As they wait for an absent one to come;
Ah! they do not know that in death, alone,
Lies " A federal soldier—name unknown."

There are loving ones who will watch and wait
For his welcome step at the garden gate ;
Yet their yearning arms will no more be thrown
'Round " A federal soldier—name unknown."

May God soothe their hearts when the war is o'er
And the father and husband come home no more.
How vain is the wife's and the mother's moan
For " A federal soldier—name unknown."

Yet the time will come, which shall re-unite
Those who pass from earth to the realm of light ;
May the loved ones meet,—at the heav'nly throne,—
With " A federal soldier—name unknown ! "

                              —*W. Dexter Smith, Jr.*

Angry Words.

Angry words are lightly spoken,
    In a rash and thoughtless hour;
Brightest links of life are broken
    By their deep, insidious power.
Hearts inspired by warmest feeling,
    Ne'er before by anger stirred,
Oft are rent past human healing
    By a single angry word.

Poison drops of care and sorrow,
    Bitter poison drops are they,
Weaving for the coming morrow

Saddest memories of to-day.
Angry words, O let them never
    From the tongue unbridled slip;
May the heart's best impulse ever
    Check them e'er they soil the lip.

Love is much too pure and holy,
    Friendship is too sacred far
For a moment's reckless folly,
    Thus to desolate and mar.
Angry words are lightly spoken,
    Bitterest thoughts are rashly stirred,
Brightest links in life are broken
    By a single angry word.

Troublesome Neighbors.

First, Mrs. McGinty came over to know
    If a pailful of coal she could borrow,
Her husband had ordered a ton from the yard;
    She'd return it by to-morrow.

Then came Mrs. Martin, from over the way,
    Who said she stepped over to see
If I would oblige her, till that afternoon,
    With only a drawing of tea.

Next came Mrs. Johnson, who'd like very much
  I'd lend her, an hour or two,
A couple of irons, as she had on hand
  Some work she hurried to do.

Then came Mrs. Thompson, a neighbor next door—
  A troublesome, cranky old dame,—
Who wanted to borrow, for that afternoon,
  The loan of my large quilting frame.

Scarce had she gone when old Widow Jones,
  Who said she was going to scrub,
Came into the room and wanted to know
  If I'd lend her the use of my tub.

Then Mrs. Wilson came over in haste,—
  In her hands a pitcher she bore;
Her molasses fell short, she hadn't enough,
  And would like to borrow some more.

Next came Mrs. Hernando, who wanted to know
  If the late paper I had read through,
And would feel much obliged to me if I would
  But loan it an hour or two.

And even at night, when going to bed,
  There came to my door Mrs. Doyle,
Who had to sit up,—her daughter was sick,—
  And wanted some kerosene oil.

With patience exhausted, I'm forced to declare
  That in future I'll lessen my labors,
By refusing to lend everything I possess
  To improvident, troublesome neighbors.
                — *Waverly Magazine.*

When Will the End Come?

When legislators keep the law,
  When banks dispense with doors and locks,
When berries, whortle, rasp, and straw,
  Grow bigger downward through the box;

When he that selleth house or land
  Shows leak in roof or flaw in right;
When haberdashers choose the stand
  Whose window has the broadest light; .

When preachers tell us all they think,
  And party leaders all they mean;
When what we pay for,—what we drink,
  From real grape and coffee-bean;

When lawyers take what they would give,
  And doctors give what they would take;
When city fathers eat to live,
  Save when they fast for conscience sake;

When one that hath a horse on sale
   Shall bring his merit to the proof,
Without a lie for every nail
   That holds the iron on the hoof;

When in the usual place for rips   .
   Our gloves are stitched with special **care**,
And guarded well the whalebone tips,
   Where first umbrellas need repair;

When Cuba's weeds have quite forgot
   The power of suction to resist,
And claret bottles harbor not
   Such dimples as would hold your fist;

When publishers no longer steal,
   And pay for what they stole before;
When the first locomotive wheel
   Rolls through the Hoosac tunnel's bore;

Till then let Cumming blaze away,
   And Miller's saints blow up the globe:
But when you see that blessed day,
   Then order your ascension robe.
               —Oliver Wendell Holmes.

Suppose?

Suppose, my little lady,
  Your doll should break her head,
Could you make it whole by crying
  Till your eyes and nose are red?
And wouldn't it be pleasanter
  To treat it as a joke;
And say you're glad " 'Twas dolly's,
  And not your head that broke?"

Suppose you're dressed for walking,
  And the rain comes pouring down,
Will it clear off any sooner
  Because you scold and frown?
And wouldn't it be nicer
  For you to smile than pout,
And so make sunshine in the house
  When there is none without?

Suppose your task, my little man,
  Is very hard to get,
Will it make it any easier
  For you to sit and fret?
And wouldn't it be wiser,
  Than waiting like a dunce,
To go to work in earnest
  And learn the thing at once?

Suppose that some boys have a horse,
  And some a coach and pair,
Will it tire you less while walking
  To say, "It isn't fair?"
And wouldn't it be nobler
  To keep your temper sweet,
And in your heart be thankful
  You can walk upon your feet?

And suppose the world don't please **you,**
  Nor the way some people do,
Do you think the whole creation
  Will be altered just for you?
And isn't it, my boy or girl,
  The wisest, bravest plan,
Whatever comes, or doesn't come,
  To do the best you can?

                                    —*Phœbe Carey.*

All's Well that Ends Well.

A friend of mine was married to a scold,
To me he came, and all his troubles told.
Said he, "She's like a woman raving mad."
"Alas! my friend," said I, "that's very bad."
"No, not so bad," said he; "for with her, true,
I had both house, and land, and money, too."

"That was well," said I.

" No, not so well," said he ;

" For I and her own brother

Went to law with one another ;

I was cast, the suit was lost,

And every penny went to pay the cost."

" That was bad," said I.

" No, not so bad," said he ;

" For we agreed that he the house should keep,

And give to me fourscore of Yorkshire sheep ;

All fat, and fair, and fine, they were to be."

" Well, then," said I, " sure that was well for thee."

" No, not so well," said he ;

" For when the sheep I got,

They every one died with the rot."

" That was bad," said I.

" No, not so bad," said he ;

" For I had thought to scrape the fat,

And keep it in an open vat,

Then into tallow melt for winter store."

" Why, then," said I, " that's better than before."

" No, not so well," said he ;

" For having got a clumsy fellow

To scrape the fat and make the tallow,

Into the melting fat the fire catches,

And like brimstone matches,

Burned my house to ashes."

" That was bad," said I.

" No, not so bad," said he ;
" For what is best,
My scolding wife is gone among the rest."

* * *

Kindly Words.

As the dew unto the floweret,
  Kindly words and kindly deed
Come unto earth's wandering children,
  To supply their spirit's need.

Kindly words make all the richer,
  Both the giver and the given,
Ever wake life's sweetest echoes,
  Making earth a second heaven.

Speak them often, speak them often,
  Do not grudge them, they may be
Life and anchor, hope, salvation,
  In some future day to thee.

We are sailing down life's ocean ;
  Oftentimes the billows roar ;
Hear ye not the waves' commotion,
  Steer ye for the heavenly shore,
Gaining glimpses of land immortal
  In eternal evermore.

Faint not, pale not, nor grow weary,
  But push onward through the strife,
Sowing goodly seeds forever,
  To spring up to perfect life.

Kindly words are full of glory,
  Glory given from above ;
Blooming maid and patriarch hoary
  Need those messengers of love.

— *Emma Passmore.*

Some One's Servant Girl.

She stood there leaning wearily
  Against the window frame,
Her face was patient, sad and sweet,
  Her garments coarse and plain ;
" Who is she, pray ? " I asked a friend,
  The red lips gave a curl—
"Really! I do not know her name,
  She's some one's servant girl."

Again I saw her on the street
  With burden trudge along ;
Her face was sweet and patient still,
  Amid the jostling throng ;
. Slowly, but cheerfully she moved,
  Guarding, with watchful care,

A market basket much too large
   For her slight hands to bear.

A man, I'd thought a gentleman,
   Went pushing rudely by,
Sweeping the basket from her hands,
   But turning not his eye;
For there was no necessity,
   Amid that busy whirl,
For him to be a gentleman
   To "some one's servant girl."

Ah! well it is that God above
   Looks in upon the heart,
And never judges any one
   By just the outer part.
For if the soul be pure and good,
   He will not mind the rest,
Nor question what the garments were
   In which the form was dressed.

And many a man and woman fair,—
   By fortune reared and fed,
Who will not mingle here below,
   With those who earn their bread,
When they have passed away from life,
   Beyond the gates of pearl,
Will meet before their Father's throne
   With many a servant girl.

Kind-Hearted George.

A poor old man sat down to eat
A little bit of bread and meat
As Georgy Wright came up the street.

His clothes were torn, his head was bare,
The wind it blew his long white hair,
As cold and friendless he sat there.

" Poor man," said Georgy with a sigh,
" I feel that I could almost cry,
You look so thin; I fear you'll die."

The old man raised his head to hear
Kind words that thrilled his heart and ear,
But down his cheek there rolled a tear.

" Alas!" he said, " If I could see
The gentle boy that speaks to me,
How very happy I should be!

" For dark to me the world has been,
And I have never, never seen
A tree, or flower, or meadow green.

" How often have I wished to view
My mother's face; the skies of blue;
And now I long to look on you."

" Poor man," said Georgy Wright, "don't cry,
But pray to God that when you die,
Your soul may go to Him on high.

" There you will see, without a tear,
Far better things than we do here,
And, oh! perhaps your mother dear."

The winning words of this dear child
Such comfort gave, the old man smiled
And felt his heavy grief beguiled.

What the Sparrow Chirps.

I am only a little sparrow,
   A bird of low degree ;
My life is of little value,
   But the dear Lord careth for me.

He gave me a coat of feathers,
   It is very plain, I know,
With never a speck of crimson,
   For it was not made for show,

But it keeps me warm in Winter,
   And it shields me from the rain :
Were it bordered with gold or purple,
   Perhaps it would make me vain.

And now that the Spring-time cometh,
    I will build me a little nest,
With many a chirp of pleasure,
    In the spot I like the best.

I have no barn or storehouse,
    I neither sow nor reap;
God gives me a sparrow's portion,
    But never a seed to keep.

If my meal is sometimes scanty,
    Close picking makes it sweet;
I have always enough to feed me,
    And "life is more than meat."

I know there are many sparrows;
    All over the world we are found,
But our heavenly Father knoweth
    When one of us falls to the ground.

Though small we are never forgotten;
    Though weak, we are never afraid;
For we know that the dear Lord keepeth
    The life of the creatures He made.

I fly through the thickest forest,
    I light on many a spray;
I have no chart nor compass,
    But I never lose my way.

And I fold my wings at twilight,
　　Wherever I happen to be ;
For the Father is always watching,
　　And no harm will come to me.

I am only a little sparrow,
　　A bird of low degree ;
.But I know the Father loves me,—
　　Have you less faith than me ?

——————•◆•——————

Smile Whene'er You Can.

When things don't go to suit you,
　　And the world seems up-side down,
Don't waste your time in fretting,
　　But drive away that frown ;
Since life is oft perplexing,
　　It is the wisest plan
　　To bear all trials bravely,
And smile whenc'er you can !

Why should you dread to-morrow
　　And thus spoil your to-day ?
For when you borrow trouble
　　You always have to pay.
It is a good old maxim,
　　Which should be often p eached,—
Don't cross the bridge before you
　　Until the bridge is reached !

You might be spared much sighing,
  If you would keep in mind
The thought, that good and evil
  Are always here combined.
There must be *something* wanting
  And tho' you roll in wealth,
You may miss from your casket,
  The precious jewel—*Health !*

And tho' you're strong and sturdy
  You may have an empty purse ;
(And earth has many trials
  Which I consider worse !)
But whether joy or sorrow
  Fill up your mortal span,
'T will make your pathway brighter
  To smile whene'er you can.
                    —*Kate Cameron.*

Little John Gay.

" No one will see me ! " said little John Gay ;
For his father and mother were both gone away,
  And he was at home all alone :
"No one will see me ! " so he climbed on a chair,
And peeped in the pantry to spy what was there ;
  Which you know he should not have done.

There stood in the pantry, so sweet and so nice,
A plate of plum-cake in full many a slice,
   And apples so ripe and so fine ;
"Now, no one will see me!" said John to himself
As he stretched out his arm to reach on the shelf,
   "This apple, at least, shall be mine!"

John paused, and put back the nice apple so red ;
For he thought of the words his kind mother had
     said,
   When she left all these things in his care ;
"But no one will see me!" thought he, "is not
     true ;
For I've read that God sees us in all that we do,
   And is with us wherever we are."

Well done! Your kind father and mother obey ;
Try ever to please them, and mind what they say,
   Even when they are absent from you ;
And never forget, that though no one be nigh,
You cannot be hid from the glance of God's eye,—
   For He notices all that you do.

Deeds of Kindness.

Suppose the little cowslip
   Should hang its golden cup,
And say, "I'm such a tiny flower
   I'd better not grow up."

How many a weary traveler
  Would miss its fragrant smell! .
How many a little child would grieve
  To lose it from the dell!

Suppose the glistening dewdrop
  Upon the grass should say,
" What can a little dewdrop do?
  I'd better roll away."

The blade on which it rested,
  Before the day was done,
Without a drop to moisten it,
  Would wither in the sun.

Suppose the little breezes,
  Upon a summer's day,
Should think themselves too small to cool
  The traveler on his way.

Who would not miss the smallest
  And softest ones that blow,
And think they made a great mistake
  If they were talking so?

How many deeds of kindness
  A little child may do,
Although it has so little strength,
  And little wisdom too.

It wants a loving spirit,
    Much more than strength, to prove
How many things a child may do
    For others by his love.

The Rain.

Millions of tiny rain drops
    Are falling all around
They're dancing on the housetops,
    They're hiding in the ground.
They are fairy-like musicians,
    With anything for keys,
Beating time upon the windows—
    Keeping time upon the trees.

A light and airy treble
    They play upon the stream,
And the melody enchants us,
    Like the music of a dream.
A deeper bass is sounding
    When they're dropping into caves,
With a tenor for the zephyrs,
    And an alto from the waves.

Oh, 'tis a storm of music,
    And Robins don't intrude
If, when the rain is weary,
    They drop an interlude.

It seems as if the warbling
　　Of the birds in all the bowers,
Had been gathered into rain drops
　　And was coming down in showers.

———————•◆•———————

The Life Clock.

There is a little mystic clock,
　　No human eye has seen,—
That beateth on—that beateth on
　　From morning until e'en ;
And when the soul is wrapped in sleep,
　　And heareth not a sound
It ticks and ticks the livelong night,
　　And never runneth down.

O, wondrous is the work of art,
　　Which knells the passing hour,
But ne'er formed, nor mind conceived
　　The life-clock's magic power.
Nor set in gold, nor decked with gems,
　　By pride and wealth possessed ;
But rich or poor, or high or low,
　　Each bears it in his breast.

When life's deep stream, 'mid beds of flowers
　　All still and softly glides,
Like a wavelet's step, with a gentle beat,
　　It warns of passing tides.

When passion nerves the warrior's arm
   For deeds of hate and wrong,
Though heeded not the fearful sound,
   The knell is deep and strong.

When eyes to eyes are gazing soft,
   And tender words are spoken,
Then fast and wild it rattles on,
   As if with love 't were broken.
Such is the clock that measures life,
   Of flesh and spirit blended;
And thus 't will run within the breast,
   Till that strange life is ended.

                   From the German.

Think Before You Speak.

A tale I will tell of a priest and his mare
As they merrily trotted along to the fair.
Of a creature more docile you never have heard;
In the height of her speed she would stop at a
      word;
And again with a word, when the rider said " Hey,"
She would put forth her mettle, and gallop away.

As along a smooth lane he quietly rode,
While the sun of September all brilliantly glowed,
The good man discovered, with eyes of desire,
A mulberry tree in a hedge of wild-brier.
High upon the boughs hung the beautiful fruit;
Its large, glossy charms might have tempted a brute·

The preacher was hungry, and thirsty to boot;
He dreaded the thorns, but he longed for the fruit.
With a word he arrested the courser's keen speed,
Then stood up erect on the back of his steed.
On the saddle he stood, while the creature kept
    still,
And he gathered the fruit till he'd eaten his fill.

" Sure, never," said he, " was a creature so rare !
How docile, how true is this excellent mare !
See, here, I now stand," and he gazed all around,
" As safe and as steady as if on the ground;
And yet how she'd fly, if some fellow this way,
Not dreaming of mischief, should chance to say
    ' Hey.' "

He stood with his head in the mulberry tree ;
And he spoke out aloud in the height of his glee ;
At the sound of his " Hey," the mare made a push,
And down went the priest in the dense brier-bush.
He remembered too late, on his sharp, thorny bed,
Much well may be thought, that should never be
    said.

All is Action, All is Motion.

All is action, all is motion,
　　In this mighty world of ours ;
Like the current of the ocean,
　　Man is urged by unseen powers !

Steadily, but strongly moving,
　　Life is onward evermore,
Still the present age improving
　　On the age that went before.

Duty points, with outstretched fingers,
　　Every soul to actions high ;
Woe betide the soul that lingers !—
　　Onward ! onward ! is the cry.

Though man's foes may seem victorious
　　War may waste and famine blight,
Still from out the conflict glorious
　　Mind comes forth with added light !

O'er the darkest night of sorrow,
　　From the deadliest field of strife,
Dawns a clearer, brighter morrow,
　　Springs a truer, nobler life.

Onward, onward, onward ever !
　　Human progress none may stay ;
All who make the vain endeavor,
　　Shall like chaff be swept away.

Yankee Doodle Junior.

Once on a time old Johnny Bull
    Flew in a raging fury,
And said that Jonathan should have
    No trials, sir, by jury ;
That no election should be held,
    Across the briny waters ;
" And now," said he, " I'll tax the tea
Of all his sons and daughters."

Then down he sat in burly state,
    And blustered like a grandee,
And in derision made a tune
    Called " Yankee Doodle Dandy."
" Yankee Doodle"—these are facts—
    " Yankee Doodle Dandy ;
My son of wax, your tea I'll tax—
    Yankee Doodle Dandy."

John sent the tea from o'er the sea
    With heavy duties rated ;
But whether hyson or bohea,
    I never heard it stated.
Then Jonathan to pout began—
    He laid a strong embargo—
" I'll drink no tea, by Jove ! " so he
    Threw overboard the cargo.

A long war then they had, in which
   John was at last defeated—
And " Yankee Doodle " was the march
   To which his troops retreated.
Cute Jonathan to see them fly,
   Could not restrain his laughter ;
" That tune," said he, " suits to a T,
   I'll sing it ever after."

With " Hail Columbia ! " it is sung,
   In Chorus full and hearty—
On land and main, we breathe the strain,
   John made for his tea-party.
" Yankee Doodle—ho—ha—he—!
   Yankee Doodle Dandy—
We kept the tune but not the tea,
   Yankee Doodle Dandy ! "

Try—Keep Trying.

Have your efforts proved in vain ?
Do not sink to earth again ;
   Try—keep trying :
They who yield can nothing do—
A feather's weight will break them through ;
   Try—keep trying :
On yourself alone relying,
You will conquer ; try—keep trying.

Falter not—but upward rise,
Put forth all your energies :
    Try—keep trying :
Every step that you progress
Will make your future effort less:
    Try—keep trying :
On the truth and God relying,
You will conquer ; try—keep trying.

Ponderous barriers you may meet,
But against them bravely beat :
    Try—keep trying :
Nought should turn you from the track
Or turn you from your purpose back,
    Try—keep trying :
On yourself alone relying,
You will conquer ; try—keep trying.

You will conquer if you try—
Win the good before you die ;
    Try—keep trying :
Remember—nothing is so true,
As they who dare will ever do ;
    Try—keep trying :   .
On yourself and God relying,
You will conquer ; try—keep trying.

Ambition, False and True.

I would not wear the warrior's wreath,
  I would not court his crown ;
For love and virtue sink beneath
  His dark and vengeful crown.

I would not seek my fame to build
  On glory's dizzy height ;—
Her temple is with water filled ;
  Blood soils her sceptre bright.

I would not wear the diadem,
  By folly prized so dear ;
For want and woe have bought each gem
  And every pearl's a tear.

I would not heap the golden chest
  That sordid spirits crave ;
For every grain by penury cursed,
  Is gathered from the grave.

No ; let my wreath unsullied be,
  My fame be virtuous youth ;
My wealth be kindness, charity,—
  My diadem be truth !

For Every One That Asketh Receiveth.

Oh, ask not wealth ;
The gaudy bauble glitters to deceive
It hath a thorn to press thee when asleep ;
It maketh wings, and leaveth thee to weep—
    Ask not what wealth can give.

Oh, ask not fame ;
The empty bubble breaks at every gale ;
Its mighty shadow stalks in midnight gloom ;
It kills its hero, then it haunts his tomb,
    Where all its triumphs fail.

Oh, ask not love ;
" The fond heart's idol " breaketh the fond heart ;
His smile is oft deceitful, and its power
Too oft is felt in sorrow's darkest hour—
    Ask not his treacherous dart.

Oh, ask not power ;
Seek not a burden that must crush thee down—
Look at the thrones of tyrants in the dust,
Behold how frail the prop in which they trust—
    Ask where their might has gone.

Ask for a quiet mind ;
A heart at rest from all the jars of strife—
A humble heart that never soars to fall—

A heart to bless the Hand that gives its all—
That priceless gift of life.

Ask for a fount of tears;
The heart to sympathize in other's woe,
The soul to feel for all the sorrowing here,
And power to point them to a better sphere,
Where tears can never flow.

Ask for a home in heaven.
Poor, lonely wanderer on life's troubled sea,
When wealth and fame and power are wrecked and
gone,
And all earth's blandishments forever flown—
Ask for a home in heaven, where grief can never
be.

Sowing and Reaping.

Go and sow beside all waters,
In the morning of thy youth,
In the evening scatter broadcast
Precious seeds of living truth.
For though much may sink and perish,
In the rocky, barren mold,
And the harvest of thy labor
May be less than thirty fold—

Let thy hand be not withholden,
　　Still beside all waters sow:
For thou knowest not which shall prosper,
　　Whether this or that will grow.
While some precious portions scattered,
　　Growing well and taking root,
Shall spring up and grow and ripen
　　Into never dying fruit.

Therefore sow beside all waters,
　　Trusting, hoping, toiling on;
When the fields are white with harvest,
　　God will send his angel down:—
And thy soul may see the value
　　Of its patient morns and eves,
When the everlasting garner
　　Shall be filled with precious sheaves.

———•◆•———

Something Still To Do.

Though the day has nearly past
　　Sit not down with idle hands,
Labor while the hours shall last,
　　While shall flow Life's golden sands;
Life is changeful, ever brief,
　　Oh! improve each fleeting span,
Turn, each day, some brighter leaf;
　　Measure Time by deeds to man.

Knows't thou not some burdened soul
   Fettered by disease and pain?
Point to him the heavenly goal,
   Bid him rise and strive again.
Knows't thou not a drooping heart
   Sinking 'neath misfortune's blight?
Go, and friendship's warmth impart,
   Give to him a ray of light.

We are not to know the way
   God shall work Life's problem out;
Let us labor while we may,
   Trusting Him, nor have a doubt.
And with love for all mankind,
   Resting not till life be through,
Let us work, when we shall find
   Something still for us to do!
               Dexter Smith.

Boys' and Girls' Rights.

In every land and continent
   Good people bear in mind,
How much is said about the rights
   Of men and womenkind;
And though we're present everywhere,
   And make a deal of noise,
There's very little said about
   The rights of girls and boys.

We want the right to use our eyes
    And take in every sight,
To see, compare, and measure facts,
    The length, and breadth, and height.
We want the right to use our tongues,
    And keep them busy, too,
In asking questions every day,
    And have them answered true.

When we do wrong, we want the right
    To claim a day of grace,
A household jury, if you will,
    To sit upon our case,
And not be punished for our faults
    With sudden words and blows,
Enough to drive the goodness out
    Through fingers and through toes.

We want to be respected, too,
    And not be snubbed outright,
And put off with a careless word,
    Because we are small and slight.
And when we take the Ship of State,
    And throw by childish toys,
We'll make a law to regulate
    The rights of girls and boys.

PART II.—PROSE.

—————◦◆◦—————

Goodness of God.

Let us consider the faculties of man, and see how many and how great are the pleasures which may be derived from them. In the family, what enjoyment do parents find in the love and care they bestow upon their children,—and how sweet and joyous is the affection which children feel towards their parents. How pleasant, too, is the love of brothers and sisters, of relations and friends.

And then, let us reflect upon the beauty that is spread over the face of nature. Why are flowers so beautiful and so greatly variegated if not to give pleasure to man? Why, if God is not benevolent, has he made hills, and valleys, and rolling waves, and rushing waters so beautiful? Why has He made the forms and motions of birds so charming, if not to give pleasure to man? If the Creator did not intend to delight us, why did He spread sublimity over the mountains and teach man to feel it? Why did he robe the heavens in azure, and make a myriad race of beings to feel their majesty and

(76)

beauty? Why did He clothe all vegetable nature in green, and make human beings with eyes to relish it above all other hues? Why did He teach the birds to sing, the waters to murmur forth melody, the trees to bend, in beauty and grace, to the pressure of the breeze? Why, if God is not a good being,—did he make this world so pleasant, endow it with light, and color, and music, and perfumes, and place beings here adapted to the appreciation and enjoyment of these things? Surely our Heavenly Father,—God,—who made all things, is infinitely wise, and great, and good, and we should ever seek to love and obey Him,—For "in Him we live, and move, and have our being."

The Flowers.

When we walk into the fields, how many flowers we behold! Some spring up in the grass, looking like little stars;—some twine in the hedge, and some hang from trees and plants.

How pleasant it is to see them with their bright and beautiful colors,—red and blue, yellow and white. Some are round like caps; some are shaped like a ball; some stand up erect, and others hang their heads,—but all are beautiful, and bespeak the power, and wisdom and goodness of our Creator.

And then while they look so fair and bright, how sweet is their fragrance! The air is full of their sweets, and the bees hum around them and sip honey from their rosy lips.

Why did God make the flowers and give to them such bright colors and such sweet odors? Was it not for our happiness?

He might have made them dull and ugly in appearance, and offensive in smell,—so that they would have given us pain instead of pleasure. But God is good, and he wished to make us happy and so he made the flowers lovely and bright.

As the sun shines upon the flowers, so our Heavenly Father will smile upon us when we do right, and try to make all about us happy.

As flowers turn towards the sun all day and seem to follow him in his course, so should we let our hearts turn to the God who made us,—for he is our bright Sun, and without him we should fade away and die.

The Clouds.

How beautiful, often, are the clouds at morn! As the sun's rays tinge them they look like ruby gems set around with gold, and the lark mounts towards them and sings as if he were at Heaven's gate.

And at noon how bright and beautiful are the clouds as, high in the sky, they float and show their pearly whiteness in the blue sky.

But at sunset the clouds are most beautiful of all, and in the far west, assume a great variety of forms and hues. At night, when the moon shines on them, they look soft, and fair, and white, and pure, —and sometimes, when all is hushed and still, they seem like a flock of little lambs asleep.

Yet, what are these beautiful clouds but vapors! How soon they change and pass away!

The life of man is like a cloud—ever fleeting and changing ; to-day it is gay and bright,—to-morrow dark, and full of gloom :—and yet again the sun's bright rays shine when it is all bright and cheerful.

As the sun gives to the clouds their beauty and brightness—gilding them with his beauty—so the smiles of our Heavenly Father cheer and bless the life of man.

It is He who gives to life's morning its bright joys; it is He who sustains and exalts us in manhood ; in the storm and darkness of life, He smiles upon us, like a rainbow, full of hope and promise ; and when death comes, if we will trust him, He will take us safely over death's cold stream, and give us a secure abode in the " house of many mansions."

Autumn,

The autumn, with its ripening fruits, and waving harvests, is now with us. We see on every hand the results of the farmer's toil and forecast in the

spring-time.   Then it was that he broke up the soil,
sowed the seed, pruned his trees, and guarded the
tender plants   Now, we see the ripening crops.
The trees are bending with the golden fruit, and
abundance rewards the farmer's toil.

But suppose the farmer had not improved the
spring time, and left the soil unturned, the seed un-
sown, the trees untrimmed, and everything neglect-
ed; what would now be the result?   We should see
nothing but barren fields, overrun with weeds and
briars ; and the farmer would feel that a winter of
want and distress was before him.

And let us remember that the autumn of life will
come on apace ; and that what we now sow, we
shall then reap. If we would reap an abundant
harvest, and gather precious fruit, and secure an
autumn of plenty and prosperity, we must now, in
the spring-time of life, be diligent and careful in the
cultivation of our hearts.   We must form only those
habits which will produce good fruits.   Our acts
must be noble, our thoughts and our words must be
pure, our feelings must be kind.   Above all we
must seek the aid of our Heavenly Father, and constantly aim to cultivate good habits.   As we now
sow, we shall then reap.   If we " sow to the wind,
we shall reap the whirlwind."

Perseverance.

"Try again," is a very useful maxim to old and young, rich and poor; and great results will come from putting this short rule into practice.

We would not give a fig for the boys and girls who sit pining and whining over an example in arithmetic, or a lesson in grammar that seems to be more difficult than common. If they will only go to work in earnest and "keep trying," all will come out right.

Let us learn a lesson from Columbus, the discoverer of America. When he first set sail, what difficulties he met with, and how often was he disappointed in his expectations! Day after day he tried and "tried again," and by perseverance he finally found the wished-for land.

But let us not forget that we may make a bad use of a good maxim, just as we may of anything else that is good. Many people have made a bad use of our maxim "Try again."

A man once made a rash leap over a large log and injured his leg. He was angry, and said, "What a fool I was to hurt me, I will 'try again.'" He did try again, and injured himself for life.

From this let us learn that we should "try again" only when the thing we wish to do is really worth doing. Let us think well of what we undertake, and if our aim is a good one, let us "try again and again," if necessary, until we finally succeed.

The Tongue.

Every child has in his mouth a thing to talk with, called the tongue. It was made to speak the truth with, and when it tells a falsehood it does that which is very wrong.

The tongue was made to speak kind and pleasant words, and when it utters unkind and harsh words it is a naughty tongue.

When the tongue says disobedient words to a father or mother, it is a wicked tongue, and when it speaks angrily to a brother or a sister, it is a very bad tongue indeed.

When the tongue uses profane, or impure words, it does that which our Heavenly Father has expressly forbidden.

And now, schoolmates, as we all have this tongue, let us ask ourselves what sort of an article it is. Does it always speak the truth? Does it always utter pure, and good words?

We are told in the Bible that the tongue is an unruly member, and let us strive earnestly to keep it in subjection,—and may it never be allowed to speak unkindly of any one, nor may it ever utter profane or impure words. If the heart is kept pure the tongue will be pure also.

Rivers.

Rivers have their rise in little rills which gush from the sides of mountains and hills. Several of these unite and form a stream ; and these streams form rivulets, and rivulets form rivers, which often run for many hundred miles, making the land upon their banks fertile.

When a river descends from high land to that which is lower, it often falls over rocks and is called a cascade, or, if very large, a cataract. Some of these are so large that their roaring noise may be heard for several miles.

Some rivers overflow their banks at certain seasons, and thus tend to make the land productive. The river Nile, in Egypt, overflows its banks and leaves a rich deposit, and very large crops of rice and grain are produced from the land. Rivers are very numerous and very useful.

Our lives may be compared to a river. The little stream is like a child, and plays among the flowers of a meadow; it waters a garden, or turns a child's mimic mill wheel. As it flows on it gathers strength, and like a child, it sometimes becomes turbulent and impatient. Sometimes, like a bad man, it causes destruction and loss wherever it goes, and becomes the terror of all. But oftentimes it flows quickly along, and, like a good man, proves a blessing in all its course.

Schoolmates, let it be our aim to resemble the river whose waters are for the good of mankind. Let our lives be so ordered that we may ever do good, and wherever we move may we cause happiness and joy to go with us:—ever looking to promote the welfare of others. Thus shall we secure the blessing and favor of our Father in Heaven.

Winter.

Cold, bustling, stormy winter is coming. The leaves have already fallen from the trees; the pretty flowers have withered; the birds have flown to warmer climes; the squirrels have gone to their nests, and soon the ground will be covered with snow, and the streams and ponds will be frozen over.

The farmer has gathered his hay and vegetables; the cattle are no longer upon the hills and in the valleys; the woodman's axe rings through the forest as he cuts the trees to supply the blazing fire. Out of doors all is dreary and cold.

But let it not be so within doors. Let us do what we can to make our homes pleasant and happy. Let us try to do something to assist the dear parents who do so much for us. Let us be kind to all, and ever seek to promote the happiness of others.

And while our hearts are thankful to our Heavenly Father for all the comforts we enjoy, may we constantly seek to do good to others, and to cheer those who are less fortunate than we.

Let us aim so to improve the spring-time of life

that its summer and autumn may abound in good fruits, and its winter be peaceful and happy.

———— ••• ————

Words of Advice.

Dear Schoolmates;—Will you allow me to give you a few words of advice, and if you will heed them I am confident you will never regret it.

Rise early, and render your thanks to the Giver of all good. Enter steadily and fearlessly upon the duties of the day. Be determined that no trial shall overcome your patience, and no impediment withstand your perseverance. If the object be worthy your efforts, let no obstacle prevent its attainment.

Never be found without an object. Ask yourself how you can do the most good; and, when you have decided, throw your whole soul into your purpose. Never do good merely to obtain praise. Take a red hot iron in your hand, rather than a dishonest penny.

Do no bad action to serve a good friend. Be indulgent to others' faults; but implacable to your own. Wage war with every evil passion, and give no quarter. Die for the truth, rather than live to uphold a lie. Never court needless danger, nor fly from a peril which duty imposes.

Read good books, select good companions, attend to good counsel, and imitate good examples. Never give way to despondency. Does the sun shine?

Rejoice. Is it covered with a cloud? Wait till the cloud has passed away.

Endeavor to add daily to your stock of useful knowledge; see that your principles and your practice are equal to your attainments.

Your deportment toward others is the standard by which they will estimate your character. Be attentive, therefore, to your manners. Those are the best manners that raise you in the opinion of others, without sinking you in your own.

In all your intercourse with others, be kind and courteous, and you will not fail to win their respect and esteem.

If you wish to become good and wise men, you must begin while you are young, or you will never begin at all.

Be Busy.

There is no better motto for us than this,—"Be busy." The young man who resolves in his youth to be always busy, will make his mark in the world. The idler never does anything; it is by the industrious, the ever busy hands and minds, that great deeds are done; and the more a man does, the more he may do. The mind grows by thought and study; by exercise, the mental, as well as the physical powers become stronger. Our country is noted for its self-made men; and why are they such? How came our lamented President Lincoln to occupy the Chair of State? He was a poor boy, without the means that many enjoy to become learned and great—with nothing but willing hands and a brave heart to make his mark in the world. These he possessed; and, with economy, industry, and perseverance, he broke down every opposing barrier, and wrote his name high on the pinnacle of fame. What he has done, others may do. Men are not born great in republican America. Americans must work out their own greatness; and activity in body, in mind, in everything, is required to do it.

The world wants just such men to live in it,—men of nerve, action, enterprise. Idlers and drones are out of place in a business world. The heavens and the earth were never intended for their habitation; let them die out! Be wide awake in spirit and in truth, is the true doctrine. The journey is before us, and if we die, we must let death overtake us scaling the rugged heights above, rather than find us wallowing in the mire beneath.

Time.

There are some insects which live but a single day. In the morning they are born; at noon they are in full life, and at evening they die. The life of man is, in some respects, similar to that of these insects. It is true he may live for years, but the time is so short, and so uncertain, that every moment is of some value. Our life may be compared to a journey. As every step of the traveler brings him nearer to his journey's end, so every tick of the clock takes us nearer to the end of life.

The life of man, like that of the insect, may be divided into three parts: youth, or morning; middle age, or noon; and old age, or evening. In youth, we get our education, and lay up those stores of knowledge which are to guide and assist us in the journey of life. As this journey is of importance, we should be busy in preparing for it. As it can be made once only, let us try to make it well. Let us see to it that the hours allotted to study or business are not spent in mere idleness. Middle age is the time for action, and in youth we should lay up knowledge, and gain wisdom that we may act well and wisely our part in later years. Youth properly improved, and middle age well spent, will tend to prepare us for old age and for the life beyond the grave. Then, schoolmates, let us all strive to be faithful in the performance of all the duties that devolve upon us, and thus gain the good will of our Heavenly Father.

The Echo.

A little boy, whose name was George, as yet knew nothing of the echo. On one occasion, when

left alone in the meadow, he cried out loudly, "O!
O!" when he was directly answered from the hill
close by, "O! O!" Surprised to hear a voice without seeing any person, he cried out, "Who are
you?" The voice replied, "Who are you?" He
then screamed out, "You are a silly fellow," and
"silly fellow" was answered back from the hill.

This only made George more angry, and he went
on calling the person, whom he thought he heard,
nicknames, which were all repeated exactly as he
uttered them. He then went to look for the boy,
in order to strike him; but he could find no one.
So he ran home, and told his mother that an impu-
dent fellow had hid himself behind the trees on the
hill, and called him nicknames. Having explained
to his mother what had taken place, she said to him,
"George, my boy, you have deceived yourself; you
have heard nothing but the echo of your own words ;
f you had called out a civil word towards the hill,
a civil word would have been given back in return."
"O," said George, "I will go down to morrow and
say good words, and get good words from the echo."

"So it is," said the mother, "in life, with boys
and girls, and men and women. A good word generally produces a good word, or, as the wise man
said, 'a soft answer turneth away wrath.' If we
smile on the world, the world will smile on us; if
we give frowns, we shall have frowns in return. If

we are uncivil or unkind towards others, we cannot expect anything better from them."

———◆◇◆———

A Psalm.

The heavens declare the glory of God; and the firmament showeth his handy-work. Day unto day uttereth speech, and night unto night showeth knowledge. There is no speech nor language, where their voice is not heard.

Their line is gone out through all the earth, and their words to the end of the world. In them hath he set a tabernacle for the sun, which is as a bridegroom coming out of his chamber, and rejoiceth as a strong man to run a race. His going forth is from the end of the heaven, and his circuit unto the ends of it; and there is nothing hid from the heat thereof.

The law of the Lord is perfect, converting the soul; the testimony of the Lord is sure, making wise the simple. The statutes of the Lord are right, rejoicing the heart; the commandment of the Lord is pure, enlightening the eyes.

The fear of the Lord is clean, enduring forever; the judgments of the Lord are true and righteous altogether. More to be desired are they than gold. yea than much fine gold; sweeter also than honey an d the honey comb. Moreover: by them is thy servant warned: and in keeping of them there is great reward·

Who can understand his errors ? cleanse thou me from secret faults. Keep back thy servant also from presumptuous sins ; let them not have dominion over me : then shall I be upright, and I shall be innocent from the great transgression.

Let the words of my mouth, and the meditation of my heart, be acceptable in thy sight, O Lord, my strength, and my redeemer.

Address of Welcome.

DEAR PARENTS AND FRIENDS :—In behalf of my teachers and schoolmates, I bid you a cordial welcome to our pleasant school-room. Here we are wont to meet, from day to day, and spend many hours in attending to those lessons which will prepare us to discharge usefully the duties of life. We have spent some of our happiest hours in this room, and have only to regret that we have not been more diligent, and more attentive to our duties as members of this school. With this regret for errors of the past, we feel a strong determination better to improve the future, so that each passing moment shall bear with it a good record.

To your attention and kindness we feel greatly indebted for the privileges we here enjoy, and we trust that we feel truly grateful. We have invited you to meet us here, with the hope that an hour may be spent which shall be mutually interesting

and profitable.   In judging of the exercises to which
you may now listen, we beg that

> " You'll not view us with a critic's eye,
> But pass our imperfections by."

We wish you to remember that we are but children, and that childhood's errors will probably mark
our performances.   We will try to feel that we are
surrounded by our dearest friends, and if we shall,
in any degree, succeed in causing the time to pass
in a manner agreeable to you, we shall feel amply
paid for all our efforts.

For myself, for my teachers, and for these my
companions, I tender you heartfelt and sincere
thanks for all past acts of favor and kindness.
Especially would we remember, with grateful feelings, those who have devoted so much time and
manifested so much interest for our good,—the
school committee.   We hope no one of them will
ever have occasion to feel that he has been dishon-
ored by the dishonorable acts of any pupil of this
school.

We have been placed under weighty obligation,
and we feel that much may justly be expected of us.
That we may properly appreciate and improve our
privileges, so that we may become intelligent, useful,
and valuable members of society, we bespeak your
continued care and watchfulness; and, in return for
them, we will endeavor so to improve our time and

opportunities as to deserve and secure your hearty approbation.

***

Don't Give Up.

If we would ever accomplish anything in life, let us not forget that we must persevere. If we would learn our lessons in school, we must be diligent and not give up whenever we come to anything difficult. We shall find many of our lessons very hard, but let us consider that the harder they are the more good they will do us if we will persevere and learn them thoroughly.

But are there not some in our school who are ready to give up when they come to a hard example in arithmetic, and say, "I can't do this?" They never will if they feel so. "I can't," never did anything worth naming; but "I'll try" accomplishes wonders. Let us remember that we shall meet with difficulties all through life. They are in the pathway of every one. We shall surely find them in the school-room, but let them not discourage us. If we will only "try and keep trying," we shall be sure to conquer and overcome every difficulty we meet with. If we have a hard lesson to-day, let us strive to learn it well and then we shall be prepared for a harder one to-morrow. And if we learn to master hard lessons in school it will prepare us to overcome the hard things that we shall meet in life, when our school days are over.

Therefore, schoolmates, let us never give up and feel discouraged because we cannot readily learn our lessons.

> " Falter not,—but upward rise ;—
>   Put forth all your energies ;
>   Try,—keep trying :
> Every step that you progress
>   Will make your future efforts less :
>   Try,—keep trying :
> On the truth and God relying,
>   You will conquer ; try,—keep trying."

A New Term.

DEAR SCHOOLMATES,—We have just commenced a new term of our school life, and we all hope it will be a pleasant and happy one. In order that it may so prove, let us not forget that much depends upon ourselves. We are assured that our kind teacher will do all in her power for our good, and that she will not ask us to do anything unreasonable.

Let us consider some of the things we must do, as members of this school, that our time may pass pleasantly and profitably.

First, we must be regular in our attendance. If we should be often absent, we should fall behind our class, and lose all interest in our studies.

We should strive to be at school, not only every day, but in season. The boy who is tardy in his attendance at school, will be very likely to be tardy in the performance of his duties when he becomes a man.

Again, it should be our aim to be industrious at school and to learn all our lessons thoroughly and at the right time. Let our motto be, " Whatever is worth doing at all, is worth doing well."

I will name only one more duty, and that relates to our deportment. If we wish to do all we can for our own good and happiness, as well as for the good of our school and the happiness of our teacher, we must be very careful of our conduct, and see that we do nothing that will disturb the school or cause our teacher pain.

I might call your attention to other particulars, but if you rightly observe what I have already named, there will be but little occasion for reminding you of other duties.

------- ◆ -------

Old Charlie.

Old Charlie was a fine-looking horse, and very spirited. He was a very strong, serviceable horse, too. But with all his good qualities, Old Charlie had one very serious fault. When placed before a light load. he was all go-ahead, and it required a strong arm to keep him in check. But when it

came to steady, hard work, then Old Charlie *would
shirk*, if he could get a chance.

I remember once father had some lumber to be
boated on the canal about twenty miles. Unable
to find a boatman, he hired a boat and took his own
team, "Old Charlie and Bill," to do the towing,
while I was driver. The horses were harnessed
tandem, that is, one placed before the other, like
most of the teams on the canal, Old Charlie being
the hind or saddle-horse. For the first two or three
miles he worked well, and then, finding it was steady,
hard drawing, he took to his old habit of shirking,
which was done so slyly that it was some little time
before I discovered it. He appeared to be drawing
hard all the time; but as the boat moved slower
than at first, and knowing Old Bill was honest and
the fault was not with him, I began to urge Old
Charlie along.

Since that time, how often have I thought of Old
Charlie when I have seen smart, active boys, and
girls too, trying to evade hard study. Such schol-
ars like easy lessons. Then they are sure to be
the first to learn them. But when the lessons need
hard study, then they seek to find some easier way
to get along. At their seats they have their books
open, and appear to be busy; but they are only
making believe. At recitation, too, how many ways
they contrive to get along, and not have it appear
that they know nothing about the lesson. If they

only made the same effort to *learn* that they do to *shirk* their lessons, they would succeed without any difficulty.

Seems to me I hear some boy or girl saying: "There, I have been acting just like Old Charlie; I have been shirking the hard work." Is that so? Then stop at once and take a new start. Press your shoulders right into the harness, and you may be sure the load will move steadily along; and before you know it your work will be done, and *well done.—Child's Paper.*

The Rain-Drop.

A little drop of rain fell into the opened leaves of a rose. It was a comfortable, cosy home for it. The bed on which it rested was soft as velvet, and the perfume of the rose was delightful. For awhile the little drop was as happy as could be.

But by-and-by it grew tired of doing nothing. It is not right, thought the little drop, that I should be idle while there is so much to do. The buds are spreading their leaves to the sun. The vines are hanging out their tiny grapes. The birds are building their nests, singing merrily while they work. The bees are flying to their hives with heavy loads of honey. Even the sunshine is warming everything into life. But I, what shall I do? I will wait and watch. The great and good God will find something for the little drop of water to do in His own good time. See, there is a cloud, no bigger than a man's hand. Some of my brothers and sisters are sleeping in it. Perhaps they will join me in a little while, and we may all work together to do something useful for this beautiful earth."

While it was speaking other clouds came up into the sky, until the heavens grew black with them. Then the rain fell merrily enough, and the little rain-drop hastened to join his brothers and sisters. Together they ran down the garden path, over the smooth sand, and then crept through the hedge and over the grass of the meadow, until, with a glad laugh, they leaped down into a brook, and sped away toward the sea. Even here the little rain-drop was not lost. It helped to water long miles of meadows and the roots of great trees in the forest. It helped turn the wheels of huge mills and factories that gave work and food to thousands. And so the little rain-drop was happy in doing good, —happier than when it nestled in the sweet, soft leaves of the rose. It became so strong that at last it swept out into the ocean to finish what it had to do. But as it went into the darkness it sang, "Happy is the little drop of water. The dear Lord did not make it for nothing. Work and sing! work and sing!"

Schoolmates,—God has something for us to do, —something higher and better than the duties of the little rain-drop. Don't wait and sleep. Learn your duties and hasten to perform them. Then will you, in due time, find your reward.

———◆◇◆———

Help One Another.

A traveler, who was crossing the Alps, was overtaken by a severe snow-storm. The cold became intense. The air was thick with sleet, and the piercing wind seemed to penetrate into his bones. Still, for a time, he struggled on. But at length his limbs became numb and a heavy drowsiness came upon him, and his feet almost refused to move, and he lay down to give way to the fatal sleep of death. But just at that moment he saw another poor traveler coming toward him whose condition was, if possible, worse than his own.

When he saw this poor man, the traveler, who just before was about to fall asleep, made a great effort. He roused himself up and crawled, for he could not walk, to his fellow sufferer. He took his hands in his own, and tried to warm them; he rubbed his body and spoke words of cheer and comfort.

As he did this, the dying man began to revive; his powers were restored, and he felt able to go forward. But this was not all;—for his benefactor, too, was recovered by the very efforts he had made to save his fellow-traveler. The exertion he had made caused the blood in his own body to circulate more freely. He grew warm while striving to warm the other. His drowsiness passed off, he no longer wished to 'sleep, his limbs recovered their strength, and the two travelers went together rejoicing on their way. Soon the storm ceased, and they reached their homes in safety.

If we feel our hearts growing cold towards others and our souls almost perishing, let us do something which may help another soul to life and make it glad. We shall find this the best way to warm, restore, and gladden our own souls.

True Courage.

True courage will make us fear to do wrong and dare to do right,—and, I am sorry to say, that many boys, as well as men, do not possess it. They fear more to face public opinion than to do wrong.

Do not be ashamed, boys, if you have a patch on your jacket. It is no mark of disgrace. It speaks well for your kind and industrious mothers. For my part, I should rather see a dozen patches on your jacket, than to hear one profane or vulgar word escape from your lips, or to smell the perfumes of tobacco in your breath. It is much better to have a patched jacket than to have a patched character.

Remember that no really good boy will shun you

or think the worse of you because you cannot dress as well as some of your companions. If a bad boy laughs at you, let him laugh and pay no attention to him. He injures himself and not you.

Many men, now rich, were once as poor as the poorest boy in this school. They were poor in property but not in character.

Fear God and dare to do right. Be honest, be kind, be faithful, and you will find friends though your clothes may be covered with patches. Fear to do wrong and dare to do right under all circumstances and in all places, and you may be sure of friends and success.

The Heavenly World.

The rose is sweet, but it is surrounded with thorns; the lily of the valley is fragrant, but it springeth up amongst the brambles.

The spring is pleasant, but it is soon past; the summer is bright, but the winter destroyeth the beauty thereof.

The rainbow is very glorious, but it soon vanisheth away; life is good, but it is quickly swallowed up in death.

There is a land where the roses are without thorns, where the flowers are not mixed with brambles.

In that land there is eternal spring, and light without any cloud.

The tree of life groweth in the midst thereof; rivers of pleasures are there, and flowers that never fade.

Myriads of happy spirits are there, and surround the throne of God with a perpetual hymn.

The angels, with their golden harps, sing praises continually, and the cherubim fly on wings of fire.

This country is Heaven; it is the country of those that are good; and nothing that is wicked must inhabit there.

This earth is pleasant, for it is God's earth, and it is filled with many delightful things.

But that country is far better; there we shall not grieve any more, nor be sick any more, nor do wrong any more; there the cold of winter shall not wither us, nor the heats of summer scorch us.

Growth.

Look at yonder spreading oak, with its massy trunk, and strong branches! Its roots strike deep into the earth. The birds build among the boughs; the cattle repose beneath its shade. The old men point it out to their children, but they themselves remember not its growth. For nearly two hundred years it has withstood the wintry tempests.

Yet that vast tree was once a little acorn,—such

as you may now find under its branches. All its massy trunk, all its knotted branches, all its multitude of leaves were in that little acorn. It grew and unfolded itself by degrees, and is now a mighty tree.

The mind of a child is like the acorn. Its powers are folded up, and do not at once appear,—but they are all there. The mind of the wisest man now living was once like that of a little child.

Instruction is the food of the mind. It is to the child what the dew, and the rain, and the rich soil were to the acorn. As the soil, and the rain, and the dew caused the acorn to grow and become a large tree, so do books and study feed the mind and cause it to expand and grow.

The acorn might have perished in the ground; the young tree might have been bent and dwarfed; —but if it grew it could not be anything but an oak.

The child may become a foolish man, but, if he lives, he must become a man. What sort of a man he shall be, will depend upon the culture he receives, and the effort he makes.

Then, schoolmates, let us cherish our precious minds, feed them with truth, and nourish them with knowledge. Our minds come from God,—made in His image. The oak may last for centuries, but our minds will endure forever.

The World.

How beautiful the world is! The green earth covered with flowers, the trees laden with rich blossoms and foliage, the blue sky, and the bright water, and the golden sunshine, all are beautiful, and great must He be who made them all.

It is a happy world. How the merry birds sing from tree to tree, and how the young lambs gambol on the hill-side. Even the trees wave, and the streams ripple in gladness. How joyfully · and proudly the eagle soars up to the glorious heavens.

> His throne is on the mountain-top,
> His fields the boundless air,
> And hoary peaks, that proudly prop
> The skies—his dwellings are.
>
> He rises like a thing of light,
> Amid the noontide blaze;
> The mid-day sun is clear and bright—
> It cannot dim his gaze.

The world is indeed a happy world, if we will drink in happiness from the various sources of God's goodness and love.

It is a great world. Look off upon the mighty ocean when the storm is upon it; to the lofty mountain when the thunder and lightning play over it; to the vast forests, to the sun, the moon, and myriads of bright stars. Is it not indeed a great and wonderful world? How great, and wise, and powerful must He be who made the world. He is truly the perfection of all loveliness, all goodness, all greatness, all gloriousness.

Let us, dear schoolmates, love and obey this great and good Being,—for in Him we live,—from Him come all our blessings.

<hr>

The Sun and Wind.

A FABLE.

The Sun and Wind once fell into a dispute as to their relative power. The Sun insisted, as he could thaw the iceberg, and melt the snows of winter, and bid the plants spring out of the ground, and send light and heat over the world, that he was the most powerful. "It may be," said he, "that you can make the loudest uproar; but I can produce the greatest effect. It is not always the noisiest people that achieve the greatest deeds."

"This may seem very well," said the Wind, "but it is not just. Don't I blow the ships across the sea, turn windmills, drive the clouds across the heavens, get up squalls and thunder-gusts, and topple down steeples and houses, with hurricanes?"

Thus the two disputed, when, at last, a traveler was seen coming along; and they agreed each to give a specimen of what he could do, and let the traveler decide between them. So the Wind began, and it blew lustily. It nearly took away the traveler's hat and cloak, and very much impeded his progress; but he resisted stoutly. The Wind having tried its best, then came the Sun's turn. So he shone down with his summer beams, and the traveler found himself so hot that he took off his hat and cloak, and so decided that the Sun had more power than the Wind.

Thus our fable shows that the gentle rays of the Sun were more potent than the tempest; and we generally find in life that mild means are more effective, in the accomplishment of any object, than violence.

What I Like to See.

I like to see a boy moving cheerfully towards the school, and quietly taking his proper place before the hour for opening school arrives. I think such a boy will make a prompt and faithful man.

I like to see a boy in his place at school every day, and never allowing himself to be absent unless he is sick. I think such a boy will make a useful and reliable man.

I like to hear a boy using kind and pleasant words to his companions. I think he will make a man whom all will be glad to meet and to regard as a friend.

I like to hear a boy speaking respectfully and

kindly of his teacher and parents. I feel that such a boy will make a good and noble-hearted man.

I like to see a boy enter the schoolroom with clean face and hands, with nicely brushed hair, and with clothes and shoes free from dirt and dust. When a man, he will be neat and tidy.

I like to see a boy who is ever ready to learn what his duties are, and ever anxious to perform them faithfully. I think such a boy will "act well his part" when he becomes a man.

And now, dear schoolmates, I am sure you will agree with me in what "I like," and may I not hope that we shall all be found striving to do those things which will be well pleasing to our dear teacher and parents, and above all to our good Father in Heaven.

I like to see a boy who dares to do right, even though his companions laugh at, and ridicule him. I think such a boy will make a true man,—one always to be trusted. Do not forget, schoolmates, that the highest kind of courage is that which makes you dare to do right. Then—

Dare to think, though others frown;
Dare in words your thoughts express;
Dare to rise, though oft cast down;
Dare the wronged and scorned to bless.

Dare forsake what you deem wrong;
Dare to walk in wisdom's way;
Dare to give where gifts belong;
Dare God's precepts to obey.

Do what conscience says is right;
  Do what reason says is best;
  Do with all your mind and might;
  Do your duty, and be blest.

What I Don't Like to See.

I don't like to see a boy idly loitering on his way to school, and coming in after the proper hour for commencing. I think such a boy, if he lives to be a man, will always be a little late in all his duties.

I don't like to see a boy sit idle in school and neglect the lessons required of him by his teacher. An idle boy will, very likely, make an idle and useless man.

I don't like to see a boy spend the precious hours of school in whispering and playing, and thus interrupting those who wish to learn. I think if he grows up he will make a troublesome neighbor.

I don't like to see a boy come to school with his face unwashed, and his clothes and shoes covered with dirt. I always think such a boy will be a disagreeable companion, and an unwelcome visitor.

I don't like to hear a boy using profane or improper language, for I fear he will, when older, form other bad habits, and become the associate of the lawless and wicked.

I don't like to see a boy with a cigar in his mouth, and forming the habit of smoking. I fear that, when a man, he will be a slave to other bad habits which will neither promote his own happiness nor add to the comfort of his friends.

I don't like to hear a boy speak harshly or unkindly to his companions. I think such a boy will become a rude and harsh man,—unworthy the friendship of the good.

I don't like to see a boy trying to get his schoolmates to help him perform his examples in arithmetic. I think he will be very apt to lean upon others for help all through life.

I don't like to hear a boy speaking unkindly of his teacher or parents. I fear such a boy is lacking in those good traits which help to make a good man.

And now I have told you of some of the things that I don't like, perhaps at some other time I will tell you of some of the things that I do like.

Selfishness.

There were once a dog and a cat sitting by a kitchen door, when the cook came out and threw several pieces of meat to them.

They both sprung to get it, but the dog was the strongest, and so he drove the cat away, and ate all the meat himself. This was selfishness; by which I mean, that the dog cared only for himself. The cat wanted the meat as much as he did; but he was the strongest, and so he took it all.

But was this wrong? No,—because the dog knew no better. The dog has no idea of God, or of that beautiful golden rule of conduct, which requires us to do to others as we would have them do to us. The hymn says,—

> " Let dogs delight to bark and bite,
>   For God hath made them so ;
> Let bears and lions growl and fight,
>   For 't is their nature to."

But children have a different nature, and a different rule of conduct. Instead of biting and fighting, they are required to be kind and gentle to one another, and to all mankind.

Instead of being selfish, like the dog, they are commanded to be just and charitable, by which I mean, that they should always give to others what is their due, and also give to others, if they can, what they stand in need of.

If a child snatches from another what is not his, he is selfish, and very wicked. If a child tries, in any way, to get what belongs to another, he is selfish, and is as bad as a thief or a robber. Selfishness is caring only for one's self. It is a very bad thing, and every child should avoid it. A selfish person is never good, or happy, or beloved.

How miserable should we all be, if every person was to care only for himself! Suppose children and grown-up people, were all to be as selfish as cats and dogs. What constant fighting there would be among them!

How dreadful would it be to see brothers and sisters snarling at each other, and pulling each other's hair, and quarreling about their food, and their playthings! We ought to be thankful that God has given us a higher nature than that of beasts, and enabled us to see and feel the duty of being kind and affectionate to one another.

And as we can see and feel this duty, we ought to be very careful always to observe it.

The Squirrel.

The more we examine the works of nature, the more we shall be made to feel that there is infinite variety in them—that almost every part of the universe is filled with inhabitants appropriate to it; and that each individual thing is fitted to the place it occupies. Among plants, for instance, there are nearly a hundred thousand kinds already recorded in the books of the botanists; among animated beings, there are, perhaps, even a greater number of species. And what a countless number of each individual kind, whether in the vegetable or animal world! Every part of the earth is occupied. The earth, the air, the sea—each and all are inhabited by myriads of living things. And how wonderfully are they all adapted to their several designs! How well is the fish fitted to his element; how admirably is the bird adapted to the life he is to lead!

Among quadrupeds, the lively little fellow, whose name we have selected for our theme, is a pleasing illustration of the success with which nature accomplishes her designs. The squirrel is made to enliven the forest, to live among woods, to gather his food, and make his nest, and spend a great part of his life amid the branches of the trees. And how perfectly is he at home in his domain! He springs from limb to limb—from tree to tree; he ascends or descends the trunk at pleasure, and seems to be as safe in his airy evolutions, as the ox, or the horse, upon the solid ground—or the bird in the air, or the fishes in the river.

How perfect an instance of adaptation is this! How nice must be a piece of machinery that could be made to operate with such celerity, in such a variety of ways, and with such certain success! And how pleasing, as an object of mere beauty, is the squirrel! How graceful his form—how cheerful his aspect—how seemingly happy his existence!

Our Conduct and Influence.

Not only for our own sakes, but on account of all with whom we associate, it is our duty to take great care of our habits. The general principle which should lead us to do this is, that we cannot live for ourselves alone. We must think of others; we must speak and act with them in our minds. And we are bound to form such habits as shall tend to their good—to make us useful in the world. We must, in a word, deny ourselves. If, while we are children, we take pleasure in giving a part of what we enjoy, be it only a bunch of flowers, or an apple, to one of our schoolmates, we shall thus prepare ourselves to make others good and happy, when we come to manhood. But a selfish habit will be very hard to change hereafter.

We should form the habit of associating with good persons. A lad may have many pleasant things about him; he may be witty, or bold, or smart; but, if he is coarse in his manners—if he is vulgar, profane, or addicted to falsehood, we should shun his company. We are apt to become like those with whom we freely associate; and although we do not mean to imitate their faults, and do not think there is any danger of it, yet we may soon fall into the same bad habits. To be safe, therefore, we should never trust ourselves unnecessarily with any but good people.

You may think it will be easy to break away from the company and acquaintance of a boy, when you find him to be very bad; but it will not be so. Many have been ruined for life by the friendships they have formed with vicious children, while at school with them. They continued to associate with them, and caught their vices in youth, and even up to manhood. If we wish to do good in the world, we must be good; and we cannot be good, if we are very intimate with bad persons.

It is our duty habitually to speak well of others. We are accustomed to do the opposite of this—to say all the bad things of others which we think the truth will allow. This is wrong. A little boy once said to his mother—"When will these ladies be gone, so that we can talk about them?" And what was to be said about those ladies? Probably the family were in the habit of speaking of the faults of their visitors. If there was anything that could be ridiculed in their dress or their remarks, then was the time to discuss it.

Now, we all know the power of habit; and if we could only learn to think what *good* things we could say of others, and keep all that was bad to ourselves, what an immense improvement there would be among school-children, and in the whole world! It is our duty to love all men; let us, therefore, try to speak well of all, and we shall soon love them. If we talk much against them, we cannot love them.

Punctuality.

We should practice punctuality for the sake of others, as well as ourselves. He who is punctual, will accomplish far more in a day than he who is not so. Washington was remarkable for this virtue. He once rode into Boston without any escort, because the soldiers were not punctual to meet him on the line at the time they promised. His mother taught him, when a boy, to have certain hours for every employment, and to do everything at the appointed time. This habit helped, in his after life, to make him a good man. He was able to do what, without it, he never could have done.

We injure others by a neglect of punctuality. A girl says to herself—"It is a little too cold, or a little too warm, to go to school to-day;" or — "I feel a slight headache;" and so she remains at home. Now, she thus not only loses all she might that day have learned, but gives her teacher trouble. He must note her absence, and when the time comes for a recitation the next day, she is behind her class, and gives him and them further trouble. We ought never to say—"It is only once—I will not do so again;" and think thus to excuse ourselves; for, from the force of habit, the oftener we are tardy, or otherwise fail in our duty, the more frequently shall we be likely to do so, and the more injury shall we do others, of course, by this fault. So that, on every account, we should be punctual.

If we form the habit of punctuality at school, it will be of great advantage to us in after life. Let us not forget that the punctual boy will be likely to make a punctual and faithful man.

Good Advice.

"Take care of the *minutes*, and the hours will take care of themselves," is an admirable remark, and might be very seasonably recollected when we begin to be "weary of well doing," from the thought of having much to do. The present moment is all we have to do with in any sense: the past is irrecoverable; the future is uncertain; nor is it fair to burden one moment with the weight of the next. Sufficient unto the *moment* is the trouble thereof. If we had to walk a hundred miles, we should still have to take but one step at a time, and this process continued, would infallibly bring us to our journey's end. Fatigue generally begins, and is always increased, by calculating in a minute the exertion of hours.

Thus in looking forward in future life, let us recollect that we have not to sustain all its toil, to endure all its sufferings, or encounter all its crosses at once. One moment comes laden with its own *little* burdens, then flies and is succeeded by another no heavier than the last; if *one* could be borne, so can another, and another.

Even in looking forward to a single day, the spirit may sometimes faint from an anticipation of the duties, the labors, the trials of temper and patience that may be expected. Now, this is unjustly laying the burden of many thousand moments upon *one*. Let any one resolve to do right *now*, leaving *then* to do as it can ; and if he were to live to the age of Methuselah, he would never do wrong. But the common error is, to resolve to act right after breakfast, or after dinner, or to-morrow morning. or *next time;* but *now, just* now, *this* once, we must go on the same as ever.

It is easy, for instance, for the most ill-tempered person to resolve, that the next time he is provoked he will not let his temper overcome him ; but the victory would be to subdue temper on the *present* provocation. If, without taking up the burden of the future, we would always make the *single* effort at the *present* moment, while there would, at any time, be very little to do, yet by this simple process continued, everything would at last be done.

It seems easier to do right to-morrow than to-day, merely because we forget, that when to-morrow comes, *then* will be *now*. Thus life passes with many, in resolutions for the future, which the present never fulfills.

It is not thus with those who, " by *patient contin-uance in well doing*, seek for glory, honor, and immortality :" day by day, minute by minute, they execute the appointed task to which the requisite measure of strength and time is proportioned ; and thus, having worked while it was called day, they at length "rest from their labors, and their works follow them."

Let us then, "whatever our hands find to do, do it with all our might," recollecting that "*now* is the proper and accepted time."

How to Have Friends.

Every child must observe how much more happy and beloved some children appear to be than others. There are children with whom you may always love to be; they are happy themselves, and they make others happy. But there are children whose society you would always avoid; the very expression of whose countenances produces unpleasant feelings; and who seem to have no friends.

No person can be happy without friends. You cannot receive affection, unless you will also give it. Hence the importance of cultivating a cheerful and obliging disposition. You cannot be happy without it. I have sometimes heard a girl say, "I know that I am very unpopular at school." Now, this is a plain confession that she is very disobliging and unamiable in her disposition.

If your companions do not love you, it is your own fault. They cannot help loving you, if you will be kind and friendly. It is true that a sense of duty may at times render it necessary for you to do that which is displeasing to your companions.

But if it is seen that you have a kind spirit; that you are above selfishness; that you are willing to make sacrifices of your own personal convenience to promote the happiness of your associates; you will never be in want of friends. You must not regard it as your misfortune, but your fault, when others do not love you. It is not beauty, it is not wealth that will give you friends. Your heart must glow with kindness, if you would attract to yourself the esteem and affection of those by whom you are surrounded.

You are little aware how much the happiness of your whole life depends upon the cultivation of an affectionate and obliging disposition. If you adopt the resolution to confer favors whenever you have an opportunity, you will surround yourself with friends. Begin upon this principle in childhood, and act upon it through life, and you will not only make yourself happy, but also promote the happiness of all within your influence.

———•••———

Habits.

When a person has done a thing several times it is easy for him to do it again. What we have often done we are very likely to repeat. This doing a thing over and over again is called *habit*—and when one of these habits become established we follow it without thinking.

Now, in fact, we are what our habits make us. If we have a good set of habits we become good, and if we have a bad set of habits they will make us bad and disagreeable.

If this is true how important it is that we be careful as to the habits we form. Let us not forget that good or bad habits, formed in youth, will very likely go with us through life.

Habits may be compared to the clothes we wear. If our clothes are good and proper, they make us attractive. If they are dirty or ragged, they will tend to make us unpleasant associates. So good or bad habits affect our character and standing. If we form and practice good habits, they will give us influence for good with the good. But if we form bad habits our influence will be with the wicked for evil. Schoolmates, will you not strive earnestly to form good habits, and avoid all that are bad?

Self-conceit.
AN ADDRESS, SPOKEN BY A VERY SMALL BOY.

When boys are exhibiting in public, the politeness or curiosity of the hearers frequently induces them to inquire the names of the performers. To save the trouble of answers, so far as relates to myself, my name is Charles Chatterbox. I was born in this town; and have grown to my present enormous stature without any artificial help. It is true, I eat, drink, and sleep, and take as much care of my noble self as any young man about; but I am a monstrous great student. There is no telling the half of what I have read. .

Why, what do you think of the Arabian Tales? Truth! every word truth! There's the story of the lamp, and of Rook's eggs as big as a meeting-house. And there is the history of Sinbad the Sailor. I have read every word of them. And I have read Tom Thumb's folio through, Winter Evening Tales, and Seven Champions, and Parismus, and Parismenus, and Valentine and Orson, and Mother Bunch. and Seven Wise Masters, and a curious book, entitled, Think well on't.

Then there is another wonderful book containing fifty reasons why an old bachelor was not married. The first was, that nobody would have him; and the second was, he declared to everybody that he would not marry; and so it went on stronger and stronger. Then, at the close of the book, it gives an account of his marvelous death and burial. And in the appendix, it tells about his being ground over, and coming out as young, and as fresh, and as fair as ever. Then, every few pages, is a picture of him to the life.

I have also read Robinson Crusoe, and Reynard the fox and Moll Flanders; and I have read twelve delightful novels, and Irish Rogues, and Life of St Patrick, and Philip Quarle, and Conjuror Crop, and Æsop's Fables, and Laugh and be fat, and Toby

Lumpkin's Elegy on the Birth of a Child, and a
Comedy on the Death of his Brother, and an Acros-
tic, occasioned by a mortal sickness of his dear
wife, of which she recovered.   This famous author
wrote a treatise on the Rise and Progress of Vege-
tation; and a whole Body of Divinity he comprised
in four lines.

I have read all the works of Pero Gilpin, whose
memory was so extraordinary that he never forgot
the hours of eating and sleeping.   This Pero was a
rare lad.   Why, he could stand on his head, as if it
were a real pedestal ; his feet he used for drumsticks.
He was trumpeter to the foot guards in Queen Betty's time; and if he had not blown his breath away,
might have lived to this day.

Then, I have read the history of a man who married for money, and of a woman that would wear
her husband's small-clothes in spite of him; and I
have read four books of riddles and rebusses; and
all that is not half a quarter.

Now, what signifies reading so much if one can't
tell of it?   In thinking over these things, I am
sometimes so lost in company, that I don't hear anything that is said, till some one pops out that witty
saying, "A penny for your thoughts."   Then I say,
to be sure, I was thinking of a book I had been
reading.   Once, in this mood, I came very near
swallowing my cup and saucer; and another time
was upon the very point of taking down a punch-

bowl, that held a gallon. Now, if I could fairly have gotten them down, they would not have hurt me a jot; for my mind is capacious enough for a china shop. There is no choking a man of my reading. Why, if my mind can contain Genii and Giants, sixty feet high, and enchanted castles, why not a punch-bowl, and a whole tea board?

It was always conjectured that I should be a monstrous great man; and I believe, as much as I do the Spanish war, that I shall be a perfect Brobdignag in time.

Well now, do you see, when I have read a book, I go right off into the company of the ladies; for they are the judges whether a man knows anything or not. Then I bring on a subject which will show my parts to the best advantage; and I always mind and say a smart thing just before I quit.

You must know, moreover, that I have learned a great deal of wit. I was the first man who invented all that people say about cold tongues, and warm tongues, and may-bees. I invented the wit of kissing the candle-stick when a lady holds it; as also the plays of criminal and cross question; and above all, I invented the wit of paying toll at bridges. In short, ladies and gentlemen, take me all in all, I am a downright curious fellow.

Boys' Pockets.

Did you ever turn a boy's pockets "inside out" and examine the contents? "Oh my! what a collection!" An old junk shop isn't a circumstance to a boy's pocket. Here you will find *buttons and cord, nails, cards, spools, tops, bits of tin, glass and leather — slate pencils, nut shells, Jews'-harps*, and a pretty good sprinkling of cake crumbs — all in a muddle. And then again notice the affection a boy has for this medley of the pocket! He watches them as a miser does his gold. If his jacket or inexpressibles have a rent in them—and you know they do *occasionally*—and they are taken for repairs, what a flutter the owner is in lest some of his precious articles get lost! O dear! what a time! Every identical thing must be turned upon the carpet—crumbs included—(much to Betty's annoyance) and the choicest ones culled out. But he never has anything to be thrown away;—not he—so there's not much left for Betty's benefit, except the aforenamed crumbs—and she never fails to grumble over them, and then she votes boys a nuisance generally. Tommy takes it all very calmly if his pocket treasures are only secured. A slight scolding does not trouble him in the least, and he always goes off whistling briskly to show his manly independence. But if anybody steals a march on him, and relieves his pockets of their extra lading, it alters the case amazingly Then, look out for a storm. It's not the least use in the world to tell him they're not good for anything—for doesn't he know better—and doesn't he want to use every one of them—some-time? So there is no peace until they are all forth-coming, and his much abused pockets are refilled. Oh boys! boys! what rude remnants of barbarism ye are! ever opposed to law and order, and wild as unbroken colts ;—

> Noisy, breezy, free and easy,
> Full of fancy, full of fun ;
> Care for mother, teasing brother,
> "Born to trouble" every one.

Let us be Friendly.

Dear Schoolmates, let us not forget that we are like members of one large family. We are sent here daily by our kind parents, that we may learn those things which we shall need to know when we become men. Our lessons may sometimes be hard, but if we are diligent and patient we shall surely learn them. As we spend many hours in every day in this school-room we ought to do all in our power to make it pleasant for each other and pleasant for our dear teacher.

Soon our school-days will be over, and if we live, we shall be men and women in the community. What kind of men and women we shall be depends very much upon how we spend our time and improve our privileges while members of this school.

Let us remember that each day has its own lessons and try to learn them well.

But most of all let us strive to form good habits, and to be kind to each other. Let us always delight to promote each other's happiness by doing kind acts and speaking pleasant words.

"Schoolmates, do you love each other?
  Are you always kind and and true?
Do you always do to others
  As you'd have them do to you?

Are you gentle to each other?
  Are you careful, day by day,
Not to give offence by actions,
  Or by anything you say?

My dear schoolmates, love each other,
  Never give another pain;
If your seat-mate speak in anger,
  Answer not in wrath again.

Be not selfish to each other;
  Never spoil another's rest;
Strive to make each other happy,
  And you will yourselves be blest."

The Blessings of Sight.

Schoolmates, do we often enough think of the many blessings for which we ought to be thankful to our Heavenly Father? We enjoy many privileges and blessings, but how seldom do we think of Him who gives them to us!

How much we enjoy from the sense of sight! But do we often enough think of those deprived of it, and how we should feel if we were denied the use of it? Let us go to some asylum for the blind. There we shall find boys and girls, no larger than we are, who cannot see a particle. They cannot see, and have never seen, father or mother, brother or sister. They cannot see, and never have seen, the sky or the clouds—or the beautiful flowers and merry birds. All this bright world is a great black space to them. As it were, they are shut up in a dark closet all the time. They cannot read as we do. They must have books with great raised letters, that they may feel them with their fingers. They must study their lessons with their fingers. When they walk, they must feel their way carefully, lest they run against something.

But we, dear schoolmates, could always see, and how thankful we ought to be for it. We have always had the most beautiful picture gallery before us, and yet how little of gratitude we have felt or expressed! Let us never retire to our beds at night without thanking our good Father in heaven for the blessing of sight.

PART III. — DIALOGUES.

Conduct.

William. Well, friend Henry, I am real glad to see you, for I have wanted to talk with you about school matters.

Henry. What is the trouble now, William? I shall be glad to hear what you have to say.

William. I have been thinking that our teacher has too much to say about our conduct—and especially about our deportment out of school. If we study well in school and learn our lessons, I think we should be allowed to do as we please afterward.

Henry. I cannot quite agree with you, William. Our deportment is of great consequence. Our teacher wishes us to behave well because it is for our good that we should do so. If we conduct ourselves properly, we shall not only be more happy ourselves but we shall make our friends happier. What are some of the things that you object to, William?

William. Why, she wishes us to be civil and orderly in the street; to use no language that we

(128)

should be unwilling to have our mothers hear, and to answer every one politely and kindly.

Henry. Why, William, I hope you do not object to these things. If you do I cannot agree with you. Our teacher wishes us to be particular in these matters because it is right for us to be so. Now, honestly, friend William, do you not think our teacher is right?

William. Perhaps she is right and reasonable— but I must say I like to do as I please when I am out of school.

Henry. We all like to do as we please, but ought it not to please us best to do what is right? If so, we can please our teacher and parents at the same time. We certainly ought to try to be good and to do good—ought we not?

William. Why — yes — but then I like to have my own way.

Henry. Very well, you can have your own way, and if that way is a good way you will be happy in it; but if it is a bad way you will not only be un-happy yourself, but you will make others unhappy also. There is Dick Lawless who has his own way to perfection; he uses wicked and improper language, runs after carriages in the street, answers people rudely, and is uncivil to everybody — and no one likes him. Now do you wish to imitate his exam-ple, and to be like him?

William. Why, no, Henry, I cannot say that I

do in all respects. I certainly would not wish to use improper language.

Henry. I am glad to hear you say so much, William. I am sure if you will properly reflect on the subject you will find that our teacher is about right, and that she is one of our very best friends. Will you not think of this?

William. Yes, Henry, I will. I confess I have not thought much about it, and what you have said makes me think that I have not felt quite right, nor acted quite right. I thank you for your friendly talk, and I certainly will consider what you have said. Good-bye.

Henry. Good-bye.

Boys' Rights.

Amos. Will, have you read what Mr. Beecher says about boys?

William. Yes! *that* I have! We gave him three times three for it. Didn't he take up the cudgel finely!

Frederic. Three times three! indeed; we gave him nine times nine! and Walton says he has a more just appreciation of boys than anybody in the world, excepting my mother, and you know every one calls her "boy-protector."

Amos. Yes! and all the boys like her, big and little.

Frederic. That's because she likes boys as well as she does girls; and other ladies *don't,* you know. They always invite the girls to the weddings and parties.

William. Yes, and when people write to my mother, to make them a visit in the country, they always say, "Bring one or two of the girls with you." The boys of course, are *welcome* to stay away!

Frederic. I know it, Will; the ladies say boys are so rude; and I think they're rude only because they know the ladies dislike them, and they think that's unjust.

William. So it is, Fred; boys are never rude to your mother. They couldn't be. She always speaks so kindly to them, and appears to have respect for them, and for what they like.

Frederic. So she has! We always expect her to take a share in all we do. We talk to her about our books, and tell her all our fun, and all our troubles, too, and she thinks as much about them as if we were grown up, and don't call them trifles.

William. I know it; I like to be at your house better than anywhere else.

Frederic. Mother often invites boys to stay there, and they always make friends with her. They're all kind to her, and try to please her.

Amos. To be sure they do; they couldn't help it if they tried.

Frederic. She says boys are a much-abused

race, and that they have rights that ought to be respected.

William. So they have! and it is too bad to be treated as all those little fellows were the other night. They went a whole hour too early, and sat waiting in that hot room, so as to get a front seat where they could see Mr. Curtis, and hear him well. Some ladies and gentlemen came too late, after he had begun to lecture, and the boys were turned out of their seats and placed where they could not see him at all.

Frederic. Mother saw it. She said she would not have taken the seat and spoiled the pleasure of the little fellows; or, if one had willingly given her his seat, she would have held him on her lap. But hasn't Mr. Beecher a good notion of what boys like? He doesn't forget he was a boy once.

Amos. No, that he don't, and we boys will not forget him. We will call him " the boys' friend,"— or the " advocate of boys' rights."

The Irish Servant.

Patrick. [*Taking off his hat and bowing.*] An' plaze yer honor, would ye be after giving employment to a faithful servant, who has been rekimmended to call upon yer honor?

Gentleman. What may I call your name?

Patrick. My name is Patrick Lynch, and I have

always been called Pat, and you are at liberty to call me that same.

Gent. Well, Pat, who was your last master?

Patrick. Mr. Jacobs, plaze yer honor; and a nicer man never brathed.

Gent. How long did you live with Mr. Jacobs?

Patrick. In troth, sir, I can't tell. I passed my time so pleasant in his sarvice that I niver kept any account of it, at all, at all. I might have lived with him all the days of my life, and a great deal longer, if I had plazed to do so.

Gent. Why, then, did you leave him?

Patrick. It was by mutual agrament. The truth was, we didn't just agree, and he said I should not live with him longer; and at the same instant, you see, I declared I would not live with him; so we parted on good terms; by agrament, you see.

Gent. Well, Pat, how old are you now?

Patrick. I am just the same age of Patrick O' Leary. He and I were born the same wake.

Gent. And how old is he?

Patrick. He is jist my age. He and I are jist of an age, you see, only one of us is older than the other; but which is the oldest I cannot say, neither can Patrick.

Gent. Were you born in Dublin?

Patrick. No, sir, plaze yer honor, though I might have been, if I had desired; but, as I always preferred the country, I was born there; and, plaze

God, if I live and do well, I'll be buried in the same parish I was born in.

Gent. You can write, I suppose.

Patrick. Yes, sir; as fast as a dog can trot.

Gent. What is the usual mode of traveling in Ireland?

Patrick. Why, sir, if you travel by water, you must take a boat; and, if you travel by land, it must be either in a chaise or on horseback; and they who cannot afford either, must trudge on foot, which, to my mind, is decidedly the safest and chapest mode of moving about.

Gent. And which is the pleasantest season for traveling?

Patrick. Faith, sir, when a man has most money in his pocket.

Gent. I think your roads are passably good.

Patrick. And ye may well say that, yer honor, if you only pay the toll-man.

Gent I understand you have many black cattle in Ireland.

Patrick. Faith, we have plenty of every color.

Gent. I think you have too much rain in your country?

Patrick. Yes, yer honor; but Sir Boyle, bless his soul, has promised to bring in an act of parliament in favor of fair weather. It was he that first proposed that every quart bottle should hold jist two pints.

Gent. As you have many fine rivers, I suppose you have an abundance of nice fish.

Patrick. And well may you say that; for water never wet better ones. Why, master, I won't tell you a lie; but, if you were at the Boyne, you could get salmon and trout for nothing; and, if you were at Ballyshanny, you'd get them for much less.

Gent. Well you seem to be a clever fellow, and, if you will call again to-morrow, I will see what I can do for you.

Patrick. I will, yer honor. Pace to your good sowl.

Doing Right.

George. I will never play with Charlie Mason again, for he is a naughty boy and I don't love him.

John. What now, George? I thought you and Charlie were great friends.

George. And so we have been, but we shall not be any longer. He caught my new ball and ran away with it.

John. But why did he do so?

George. Why, we were playing, and he asked me to let him take it. I told him I did not like to lend it, and pretty soon when it bounced over his way he caught it and ran home with it.

John. Well, it was wrong for Charlie to take it in that way. But if he had a new ball, would you not like to take it for a while?

George.   Certainly, I would.

John.   And don't you think he would let you take it?

George.   Why, yes, I guess so ; for Charlie is a very good boy sometimes.

John.   Well, George, do you remember that the golden rule says we must do to others as we would like to have them do to us? You say that you would much like to play with Charlie's ball, and yet you are not willing he should play with yours. This is not doing as you would be done by. You have both done wrong.

George.   But Charlie has my ball, and he has no right to keep it.

John.   Well, he will return it to you soon, I have no doubt.

George.   He had no right to take it, and surely he did not do to me as he would have me do to him.

John.   I suppose he did not consider anything about it,—any more than you did in not letting him play with you. But don't you remember how kind Charlie was, a short time ago, when he had his new balloon? Did you not play with it?

George.   O yes! and I let it blow away into a big tree, and Patrick could not get it again.

John.   And did Charlie cry about it?

George.   No, but he was very sorry, and so was I. I took the money uncle gave me and bought some paper, and sister Mary made him a new balloon.

John. And did you not feel happy when you carried it to him? And was not Charlie very glad to have it?

George. Yes, indeed, he was, and he has it now, and sometimes we play with it.

John. That was doing right. You lost his balloon and gave him another.

George. If Charlie loses my ball do you think he will do right and bring me another?

John. Certa'nly, he will, if he is a good boy, as I think he is.

(Enter Charlie.)

Charlie. Here is your ball, George. I did wrong to take it away, and I am very sorry I did so. I hope you will forgive me.

George. O, certainly, I will; and I am very sorry I refused to let you take the ball. I will try to be better hereafter, and practice the golden rule.

Charlie. That's just what I mean to do:—so we will be good friends—as we always have been.

————•••————

About School.

Henry. William, I am glad to see you, for I want to have a little talk with you about our school. Don't you think we have a very good teacher, and a very pleasant school?

William. No, I am sure I do not. I perfectly hate school and all that belongs to it. I might like it well enough if we had a different teacher.

Henry. Why, William, how can you speak so ! For my part I think we have a very kind and faithful teacher. I am sure she tries hard to teach us.

William. Well, perhaps she does ; but she is so very particular and strict that we cannot have a bit of fun.

Henry. We do not come to school for the sake of fun, but we come to learn those lessons which will prepare us to " act well our parts in life."

William. It may be well enough to learn some lessons, but what is the use of being so very strict and particular ? I can't see any harm in whispering and laughing, but if I only speak a word the teacher gives me a check and I have to stay after school.

Henry. But you must remember, friend William, that we cannot work and play at the same time. If we wish to study and learn our lessons, it is very important that we have a quiet school room. If all the pupils should do as you wish to do, and whisper and laugh whenever they pleased, we could not learn anything. Our teacher is particular for our good, and not for the sake of troubling us. Would you really like to attend school where the teacher would allow the pupils to do as they please ? Would not such a school be all in confusion ?

William. It might be all confusion, but it would suit me well enough. I like to have a lively time.

Henry. So do I like to have a lively time, but not at an improper time, nor in the wrong place.

Our parents and friends furnish us with a good school, and give us the time to attend the same,— not that we may play, but that we may learn. Now, William, do you think it is treating them properly if we spend our time in the school-room in laughing and playing? Are we not ungrateful, to say the least?

William. I had not thought of that before, and I must confess that it is not quite right to waste or misuse our time, as I have done. I thank you, Henry, for your kind words, and I hope I shall do better in the future. Certainly, I will try to do so.

Henry. Good for you, William, and if you will only persevere you will find our school and teacher all right, and you will enjoy coming to school as you have never done before.

———•♦•———

Don't Be too Positive.

Sarah. Mother, may I go and spend this afternoon with Mary Smith?

Mother. How do you know she will be at home, and that she will wish to see you?

Sarah. Because, mother, she asked me to come, and said she should be at home and that we would have a nice time.

Mother. When did she ask you, Sarah?

Sarah. Yesterday—yes, yesterday afternoon.

Mother. Are you sure, my daughter, that it was yesterday?

Sarah. Yes, mother, I *am* sure. I saw her on the green, near the school-house. We had quite a pleasant talk, and I am certain it was yesterday — just as certain as can be. Why, mother, how could I be mistaken? I *know* it was yesterday, — and in the afternoon—soon after dinner.

Mother. That cannot have been, Sarah, for I have just come from Mrs. Smith's, and she told me that Mary went to Boston on the morning train yesterday.

Sarah. Oh! well, — come to think of it, it was not yesterday, but day before. Yes, now I remember, mother, it was day before yesterday. She was going to Boston in the morning and return in the afternoon.

Mother. Well, my child, I am very sorry to see you so very certain—so *positively* sure, when really you are not sure, but wrong in your impression. You must learn to be more careful. I shall let you go and see Mary, and, as you walk along, reflect upon your error, and hereafter be very careful and not be *too positive.*

Sarah. Thank you, mother; I will not forget what you say.

Fortune Telling.

George. I wish I had a book which they sell at the stores for telling one's fortune.

William. O! so do I. They say they are very nice indeed, and that from them you can learn what your fate will be. It will tell all about our future.

George. That is so, — and I mean to get one as soon as I have money enough, — and then I can learn what my luck is to be.

Amos. Why, boys, I have a book that will tell your fortunes, and very correctly, too.

George. You have one? Why did you not tell us before? Where is it? Do let us see it. I am quite impatient to know what my fortune is to be.

Amos. Well, I will let you see mine, sometime.

William. And will it really tell what will come to pass, Amos, or are you only fooling us?

Amos. What it says may be relied on, — and it *will* tell us what will come to pass.

George. But how do you know that? You have not lived long enough to know if it has told your fortune right.

Amos. Not mine, it may be true, yet. But it is a very old book. My grandfather owned it, and he said it told the truth, and my father had it and it proved itself true to him.

William. Well, now that beats all I ever heard. It must be a prize. Why don't you take it and go around telling fortunes? You would make lots of money.

Amos. But I am afraid people would be slow to believe me, even though I should predict truly concerning them.

George. Will you sell it to me, Amos? If you will I will see what I can do with it.

Amos. I cannot sell it. It was a present from my dear father, and I would not part with it for any sum.

William. Well, you will let us see it, won't you?

Amos. Certainly, I will, and I can tell you where you may get one like mine.

George. Let us see yours first, and if that tells us the truth we will buy one for ourselves.

Amos. If you will wait here a few minutes I will get mine and read some of it to you.

(Goes after the book.)

William. George, I can hardly wait till he returns, — but I suppose he will not be gone long. There, — he comes now, with the book in his hand.

Amos. This is the book, and I will read from it, and what it says you may be sure will come to pass.

(Amos reads.)

" He becometh poor that dealeth with a slack hand; but the hand of the diligent maketh rich."

"The fear of the Lord prolongeth days; but the years of the wicked shall be shortened."

"There shall no evil happen to the just; but the wicked shall be filled with mischief."

"He that walketh with wise men shall be wise; but a companion of fools shall be destroyed."

"A soft answer turneth away wrath; but grievous words stir up anger."

"He that covereth his sins shall not prosper."

"A wise son maketh a glad father; but a foolish son is the heaviness of his mother."

"And we know that *all things* work together for good to them that love God."

All these and many other predictions are in the book, and they have always proved true and they always will.

William and George. Do tell us the title of the book that we may get one for ourselves.

Amos. It is called "THE BIBLE," — and if you will read it carefully. you will find it is the best fortune telling book in the world: — indeed, it is the only reliable one.

———•◆•———

Strict Honesty.

Sarah. I say, Jane, just bring me a sheet of writing-paper, will you? for I must write a letter.

Jane. Where am I to find it?

Sarah. Why there's plenty in my mistress's letter-case in the parlor.

Jane. Yes; but that is not mine, nor yours either.

Sarah. Well, what does that signify? I am sure there is plenty; my mistress will never miss it; and what's the value of a sheet of paper?

Jane. Why, whether my mistress should miss it or not, makes no difference at all. It is not mine, and I cannot take it; it is not honest.

Sarah. Honest, indeed! Well, I never was suspected of being dishonest in my life; and I lived four years in my last place, and I had a good character for honesty when I came away, and I never scrupled to take a trifle of that kind either.

Jane. It seems then your mistress did not know that these trifles were taken, or perhaps the character she gave you might have been different.

Sarah. Why, as to that, what is the value, I say, of a sheet of paper? My mistress can afford *that* well enough, I warrant you.

Jane. Why, now, it seems to me that the value of the thing signifies nothing; the question is whether it is *mine*, or whether it is not; and if it is not, I have no business to lay a finger on it. Besides, I look upon it, that when we take a little thing because we think it will *not* be missed, it is a sign that we only keep our hands from greater things because we think they *will* be missed.

Sarah. Nay, I think I would not take a great thing either.

Jane. Why not?

Sarah. I don't know.

Jane. No; but depend upon it that, if you have a right principle, it will keep you from small crimes as well as great ones. You remember the verse that our old dame taught us at school:

> " It is a sin to steal a pin,
>   Much more to steal a greater thing."

And we have been taught to keep "our hands from picking and stealing." And though, perhaps, we may do these things without being seen, that does not turn wrong into right. Besides, those who do these things, always take care to do them when their masters and mistresses do not see them. Now, if they did not know that they were doing wrong, they would not be ashamed of being seen. We may be pretty sure that, when we are afraid of being seen, we know that we are doing what we ought not to do.

Sarah. Well, I believe you are right; but I cannot help often thinking that you are too particular. Why, the other day, when a few little sweet cakes came out of the dining-room after dinner, you would not as much as give me one, and I dare say you would not touch one yourself.

Jane. I could not give you one, Sarah, for they

were not mine; and, for the same reason, I, of course, could not touch one myself.

Sarah. Why, they never would have been missed; neither master nor mistress would have counted them. If I had thought they would, I would not have touched one for the world; for they never would have believed me to be honest again; and, with a servant, *character* is everything.

Jane. Why, to be sure, to a servant *character* is a great thing; but, I think, *principle* is a greater. If we forget what is the right principle to act upon, and only think of character, I doubt not there will be many a time when the temptation to do wrong will lead us astray, when we think that nobody is looking on; therefore the Scripture rule, " Thou, God, seest me," is always the right rule in great things as well as little.

Sarah. Why, that is true, to be sure. And as to taking a little cake or so, I do remember that Betty Wilkins took one, and her master found her out, for he had long thought that the little things disappeared by degrees; and so he really did count the cakes that went out one day after dinner, and one was gone; and so Betty, who had the care of them, was found out and turned away. The master said he did not care a pin about the value of the cake, but he never could feel comfortable in trusting anything to her care again.

Jane. Why, I think *every* master must feel so.

Let you and me, Sarah, always keep on the right side, and then we need not mind who sees us. Let us be careful not to do wrong, and then we need not fear being found out.

Sarah. I know your advice is good, Jane, and if we were all to keep it, it would be much better for us, and we should be much happier; but, you know very well that servants do a hundred little things that they would not wish their masters or mistresses to know of.

Jane. I know very well that a truly honest servant would do nothing that she would be afraid to have known; and whatever others may do is no rule at all to us. Our rule must be to do *right*, and may God's grace enable us to walk by this rule.

On Language.

Mamma. What book are you reading, Charles?

Charles. Bingley's Animal Biography, mamma.

Mamma. Show me what part you were reading; and tell me if you quite understand it.

Charles. Nearly all of it, mamma.

Mamma. I wish you, my dear, never to pass over a single word which you do not understand. Always ask for an explanation of it.

Charles. Here is the place in the book, " The Antelope tribe."

Mamma. We will take this, then, for our lesson. Read it, Charles, one sentence at a time.

Charles. "The antelopes are, in general, an elegant and active tribe of animals, inhabiting mountainous countries, where they bound among the rocks with so much lightness and elasticity, as to strike the spectator with astonishment."

Mamma. Stop there, Charles. What is the Antelope?

Lucy. An animal.

Mamma. Of what class?

Fanny. A quadruped.

Mamma. What is meant by saying, "they are *in general* active, etc?"

Charles. That they are most commonly so.

Mamma. You are right. What do you mean by "elegant"?

Charles. Graceful, well made, full of grace.

Mamma. Can Lucy tell me what 'active' means?

Lucy. Lively, moving about a great deal.

Mamma. And what does a "tribe" mean?

Fanny. A class, a race of beings.

Mamma. Give me an instance by which this can be proved.

Charles. Oh, mamma, the hymn we transposed yesterday,

> 'Let every nation, every tribe
> On this terrestrial ball,' etc.

Mamma. What part of speech is 'active?'

Fanny. An adjective.

Mamma. Lucy, tell me what your sister means by an adjective?

Lucy. A word added to a noun, to show its quality.

Mamma. Which is the noun, then, here?

Lucy. 'Tribe,' mamma.

Mamma. What does 'an animal,' mean?

Charles. Any living thing.

Mamma. This is not a sufficiently clear definition.

Fanny. No,—because plants are alive; but they are quite different from animals.

Mamma. What distinguishes an animal from a plant?

Charles. The one can move itself where it pleases, and the other cannot.

Mamma. Yes; life is distinguished into animal and vegetable life. How will you define the difference between them?

Fanny. Vegetable life is shown by plants growing gradually larger, and producing seeds, from which other plants spring; and animal life is shown, as Charles said, by those who possess it being able to go from one place to another.

Mamma. Yes, and by what is called volition, that is, the exercise of will. We will now go on. Explain the word 'inhabiting.'

Fanny. Dwelling, or living, or existing in.

Mamma. 'Mountainous countries.'

Lucy.   Countries full of mountains.

Mamma.   What would be the opposite to a mountainous country ?

Fanny.   A flat country.

Mamma.   Give me another word, Charles.

Charles.   A level, or even country.

Mamma.   What do you mean by ' a country ?'

Lucy.   Land, mamma.

Mamma.   Your papa has land, has he, therefore, a country ?

Lucy.   No, he has not; his is only an estate.

Mamma. You must then give me a clearer explanation of the word country.

Fanny.   A large tract of land joined together, and generally containing rivers and hills.

Mamma.   That is better, but how do you distinguish this from a county ?

Charles.   Oh, a county is much smaller, mamma, it is a subdivision of a country.

Mamma.   These antelopes 'bound ;' what does that mean ?

Fanny.   Jump, spring, leap.

Mamma.   'Among ?'

Charles.   There it means, about and between, and upon.   I do not know *one* word that will express it.

Mamma.   I think I know one beginning with A which is better than yours, Charles.

Fanny.   Amidst, mamma: am I right ?

Mamma. Yes, Fanny. What am I to under-stand by 'a rock?'

Lucy. A very high, large place.

Mamma. Then our house is a rock, Lucy, it is both high and large?

Lucy. Oh, no, mamma; a rock is a natural thing, and our house is an artificial thing.

Mamma. Right, my dear; I am glad you have remembered the meaning of those words; but if you allow yourself time to think, you can give me a clearer idea of a rock than you have done.

Lucy. It is high, like a hill, only stony, instead of earthy.

Mamma. That is much better, Lucy; what are its qualities?

Lucy. Hard, and cold, and craggy, and sharp.

Mamma. What does 'lightness' mean, Lucy?

Lucy. I suppose it means that it does not jump heavily and awkwardly.

Mamma. Just so; now for 'elasticity?'

Fanny. It means, does it not, that it springs easily?

Mamma. It does; an elastic thing, when bent, returns easily to the same place again. Tell me the names of some things that are elastic?

Lucy. A bow, mamma.

Mamma. Now, another instance.

Charles. India rubber.

Mamma. That is a very good illustration; think again.

Fanny. A watch spring.

Mamma. Now another.

Charles. A branch of a tree; for, if you bend it down, it recovers itself instantly.

Mamma. Very true. Is 'to strike' a noun, Lucy?

Lucy. No, mamma, a verb.

Mamma. Why so?

Lucy. Because it expresses action. To *strike* is an active verb.

Mamma. And its meaning is to give a blow?

Fanny. Sometimes, mamma; but in this instance it means to make a person feel anything suddenly. That is a blow to the *mind*, is it not?

Mamma. You are right; and 'astonishment' means—

Charles. Surprise, wonder.

Mamma. And 'a spectator' means—what Fanny?

Fanny. A person who sees anything done.

Mamma. But in one word, my dear?

Fanny. A beholder; an observer.

Mamma. We have now got at the meaning of all these words; tell me what you have understood by the sentence. Of what is it speaking?

Lucy. Of antelopes.

Mamma. What description is given of them?

Fanny. That they are elegant and active.

Mamma. What feeling do they give to a spectator?

Lucy. They fill him with wonder.

Mamma. Why do they do so?

Charles. Because they bound about the rocks with so much agility.

———•◆•———

Punctuality.

Lizzie. Good morning, Helen.

Helen. O, Lizzie! I am so glad to see you! I did not know whether you would call for me or not. I've asked you to so many times, and you never did it.

Lizzie. Well, I promised to this time, if you would promise to be ready. I always keep my promises, but I see that you have not kept yours.

Helen. O, I am almost ready. I have only my bonnet and cloak to put on. But how do you manage to come along so early in the morning? It is not ten minutes since I finished my breakfast.

Lizzie. It is not? Why we had our breakfast an hour ago.

Helen. When did you dress, I'd like to know?

Lizzie. I dressed before breakfast. That is the way I always do. Don't you?

Helen. No, indeed! Our girl won't get up early enough; mother always tells her to get us up in time for me to go to school, but she don't get our room warm enough for us to be up before the breakfast-bell rings, and then, of course, I'm not ready for school.

Lizzie. Yes, I suppose she has a fire to make in your room, one in the dining room, and one in the kitchen ; and then, when she gets breakfast ready, you are not ready to eat it. I do not think it is her fault if you are late.

Helen. Well, one can't get up in a cold room these freezing mornings ;—but where are you going?

Lizzie. I am going to school, or I shall be late too.

Helen. Wait just a minute. I have only my gloves to put on. O, yes! and there is my library book ! I do believe that I have not chosen my numbers yet for another. Come, Lizzy, sit down and write them off for me while I find my gloves. There's a good girl.

Lizzie. I don't know what to write for you, so it would be of no use to wait. And then you have your gloves to find, and your rubbers to warm and put on, and your cuffs ;—I must go ; good-bye !

Helen. O, now, Lizzy ! I should think if you loved me you might wait just a minute; I don't like to go alone.

Lizzie. But, Helen, if you loved me, you surely would not want to make me late to school, when I can't do you any good by waiting? Just think how you would like to be kept out late, after getting up so early and trying so hard to be in season. Now you must not be angry with me; I'll talk it all over with you some other time. Goodbye.

(*Helen retires. Frances comes in.*)

Frances. My dear Lizzy, I'm afraid we shall be late.

Lizzie. So am I; but I really could not help it. And I am afraid that my dear Helen will not forgive me for not waiting still longer for her.

Frances. Wait for her? Why, she is always late. Does she want to make you late too?

Lizzie. You see, Frances, that she does not know how pleasant it is to be punctual. She is not there to see. I would not miss the bright smile and kiss of my teacher for anything.

Frances. Your teacher kisses those that come late too, doesn't she?

Lizzie. Yes, but somehow she does not look right into their eyes so sweetly, nor grasp their hands so warmly. O, Frances, I do think that I have the best teacher that ever lived.

Frances. Well, my teacher is not always there in season; but I come early so as to get the tickets. I don't believe that Helen ever gets any tickets.

Lizzie. No; she says that she does not care for them; but, for my part, I think that I should like to come early if my teacher did not, and if there were no tickets given out.

Frances. Well, I don't know; I don't see why you should.

Lizzie. O, I always feel so much happier, because it is right. I feel just as if God is better pleased with me if I am in season; and though I wanted very much to please Helen by waiting for her, yet I thought I could not afford to displease God for the sake of pleasing her. But here we are at school.

Frances. Well, I suppose you are right; but here we are. The teacher is just getting up to read the hymn. In a minute more those cards would have been turned, and we would be obliged to to read the odious words, " I am late."

Haughtiness Rebuked.

Thomas. I don't see why it is, George, that you call Colman Cutler the best boy in school.

George. Surely he is the best scholar. Who else is so correct in his lessons and so prompt in his recitations? He never fails,—and is always ready.

Thomas. Ready enough it may be, but he is not always at the head of his class. I am there quite as often as he is.

George. Very true. — you are there sometimes,

but how do you get there? Is it by hard study,—
or because you take a sly peep into your book?

Thomas. Who says I do so?

George. Who says so? Why, don't we all see
you! It was really funny the other day to hear
you answer the wrong question,—and we could not
help laughing when the master said you would have
done nicely had it happened to you to answer the
next question. Colman got above you that day, and
he will not very soon lose the place.

Thomas. That's nothing. It does not prove him
to be the best scholar. He is by no means much of
a gentleman.

George. A school boy hardly claims to be much
of a gentleman,—but Colman is a very polite and
civil boy. He is always very kind, and ready to
do a good act for any of his schoolmates.

Thomas. What of that? That does not prove
that he is a gentleman or a gentlemanly boy. Just
look at his clothes—do look at his clothes! No
tailor ever made them. They don't fit like my
clothes.

George. That's a good one! As if the set of
one's clothes made the gentleman.

Thomas. I did not mean the set alone; but his
clothes are coarse, and even patched. Just look at
my clothes! I wear the best cloth of any boy in
school;—and I carry a watch too.

George. And hence you think you are the first scholar—hey, Thomas?

Thomas. I said no such thing. But I heartily despise patched clothes, and scorn those who wear them.

George. Well done! Then you must scorn me and nearly every other scholar in school. But I don't care. Nobody can play much without having a patch now and then. But, Thomas, let us go and play now.

Thomas. No, George, I am not going to play: I have no time to play; but your precious Colman has time for everything.

George. That is very true, though you speak sneeringly. He knows how to take care of the minutes. Our teacher told us the other day that if we took care of the minutes we should have time for everything. She said that "drops make the ocean, and minutes make the years,"—and I shall try to remember it.

Thomas. You can remember what you please. For my part, I do not care to remember anything that our teacher says,—or that you say,—or that your friend Colman says either.

George. Come, Thomas, don't be fretful. Let us go upon the play-ground and have a good time.

Thomas. Not I. You don't catch me playing with boys who wear patched clothes.

George. Very well, if you prefer not to go, we

can get along without you. I trust that you will at some time learn that real worth and goodness may exist under patched clothes as well as under the richest broadcloth. Remember that *worth* makes the man—the want of it, the fellow.

———◆•———

On Politeness.

Martha. Good morning, cousin Mary. I am glad to see you, for I have something to say to you. Julia and I have been talking very earnestly on a subject, and we became almost angry because we differed in opinion. I have been longing to see you that I might know your feelings on the subject,—and I am quite sure you will be on "my side."

Mary. I should certainly be very sorry not to agree with you. I believe you and I think alike on most matters, and I hope we may now. Pray what subject has provoked so much excited feeling? Some new style of bonnet or dress, I imagine.

Martha. O no! cousin Mary, neither of these. We have been talking of the manners of two of our schoolmates—Sarah Wilson and Jane Smith. Julia prefers Sarah's manners, and I prefer Jane's. So there we differ. Julia thinks Sarah is a perfect pattern of propriety, and I don't think so.

Mary. But what makes Julia think so?

Martha. Because Sarah always smiles so sweetly when she speaks;—always shakes hands with people ; flatters them, and tells them of compliments she has heard of them,—and all that sort of thing.

Mary. Is Sarah the same to all, cousin Martha?

Martha. Oh, no:—she is polite only to a certain set of people,—those she happens to fancy. But Jane is just the same to all,—rich or poor. I think true politeness requires us to treat all with respect and courtesy. Genuine politeness must spring from a kind and generous heart.

Mary. I agree with you there, Martha. This very day I saw illustrations of true and false politeness. As I was riding in the omnibus this morning, there were two well dressed young men. One of them was very polite to a nicely dressed young lady opposite him. If, by mere accident, he touched the hem of her dress, he made a very gracious apology, and the other passengers evidently regarded him as a model of politeness. The other young man was well dressed and quiet. Suddenly the omnibus stopped to take in an old lady who had with her a large bundle—and as the carriage was crowded she was obliged to hold the bundle. She looked feeble and fatigued, and, as the last named young man saw her, he kindly offered to take her bundle. At this, the young man and young lady first named exchanged smiles and cast contemptuous glances at the young man with the bundle. The poor woman evidently noticed their conduct. However, she did not ride far, and when the omnibus stopped,—the young man very kindly assisted her out, and with as much attention as though she had been a lady of high rank. I was greatly pleased, and made up my mind that the young man possessed genuine politeness.

Martha. Well, now, your case is precisely like mine. I think Sarah aims to be polite to a certain class whom she regards with especial favor, while she treats others very coolly, not to say very impolitely. But Jane is kind and pleasant to all, and wherever she is she succeeds in making those around her happy.

Mary. Very well, cousin Martha, I now understand your position, and I do most sincerely agree with you. As we both agree that Jane's conduct and manner is far preferable, let us both try to take her for our model. One who is truly kind and polite to all must enjoy the highest kind of satisfaction, for such an one may well feel that he is acting in accordance with the wishes of our good Father in Heaven. Let us remember that true politeness comes from the better and nobler impulses of our natures and requires that we should treat *all* with kindness and true courtesy.

Hard to Please.

Mr. Cross. Why do you keep me knocking all day at the door?

John. I was at work, sir, in the garden. As soon as I heard your knock, I ran to open the door with such haste that I fell down.

Mr. C. No great harm was done in that ! Why didn't you leave the door open ?

John. Why, sir, you scolded me yesterday be-because I did so. When it is open, you scold; when it is shut, you scold. I should like to know what to do.

Mr. C. What to do ? What to do, did you say ?

John. I said it. Would you have me leave the door open ?

Mr. C. No.

John. Would you have me keep it shut.

Mr. C. No.

John. But, sir, it must be either open or—

Mr. C. Don't presume to argue with me, fellow ?

John. But doesn't it hold to reason, that a door—

Mr. C. Silence, I say !

John. And I say that a door must be either open or shut. Now, how will you have it ?

Mr. C. I have told you a thousand times, you provoking fellow—I have told you that I wished it—but what do you mean by questioning me, sir ? Have you trimmed the grape-vine, as I ordered you ?

John. I did that three days ago, sir.

Mr. C. Have you washed the carriage ?

John. I washed it before breakfast, sir, as usual.

Mr. C. You idle, negligent fellow!—you have'nt watered the horses to-day!

John. Go and see, sir, if you can make them drink any more. They have had their fill.

Mr. C. Have you given them their oats!

John. Ask William; he saw me do it.

Mr. C. But you have forgot to take the brown mare to be shod. Ah! I have you now!

John. I have the blacksmith's bill, and here it is.

Mr. C. My letters—Did you take them to the post-office? Ha! You forgot that,—did you?

John. Not at all, sir. The letters were in the mail ten minutes after you handed them to me.

Mr. C. How often have I told you, sir, not to scrape on that abominable violin of yours? And yet this very morning, you—

John. This morning? You forget, sir. You broke the violin all to pieces for me last Saturday night.

Mr. C. I'm glad of it!—Come, now; that wood which I told you to saw and put into the shed,— why is it not done? Answer me that.

John. The wood is all sawed, split, and housed sir; besides doing that, I have watered all the trees in the garden, dug over three of the beds, and was digging another when you knocked.

Mr. C. O, I must get rid of this fellow. He will plague my life out of me. Out of my sight sir!

The Colonists.

Mr. Barlow, Arthur, Beverly, Charles, Delville, Edward, Francis, George, Henry, Jasper, Lewis, Maurice, Oliver, Philip, and Robert.

Mr. Barlow.   Come, boys, I have a new play for you.   I will be the founder of a colony ; and you shall be people of different trades and professions, coming to offer yourselves to go with me.—What are you, Arthur ?

Arthur.   I am a farmer, sir.

Mr. B.   Very well.   Farming is the chief thing we have to depend upon.   The farmer puts the seed into the earth, and takes care of it, when it is grown to the ripe corn ; without the farmer we should have no bread.   But you must work very hard ; there will be trees to cut down, and roots to drag out, and a great deal of labor.

Arthur.   I shall be ready to do my part.

Mr. B.   Well, then, I shall take you willingly, and as many more such good fellows as you can find.   We shall have land enough ; and you may fall to work as soon as you please.   Now for the next.

Beverly.   I am a miller, sir.

Mr. B.   A very useful trade !   our corn must be ground, or it will do us but little good.   What must we do for a mill, my friend ?

Bev.   I suppose we must make one.

Mr. B. Then we must take a *mill-wright* with us, and carry mill-stones. Who is next?

Charles. I am a carpenter, sir.

Mr. B. The most necessary man that could offer. We shall find you work enough, never fear. There will be houses to build, fences to make, and chairs and tables besides. But all our timber is growing; we shall have hard work to fell it, to saw boards and planks, to hew timber, and to frame and raise buildings.

Charles. I will do my best, sir.

Mr. B. Then I engage you; but you had better bring two or three able hands along with you.

Delville. I am a blacksmith.

Mr. B. An excellent companion for the carpenter. We cannot do without either of you. You must bring your great bellows, anvil, and vise; and we will set up a forge for you, as soon as we arrive. By the by, we shall want a mason for that.

Edward. I am one, sir.

Mr. B. Though we may live in log houses at first, we shall want brick-work, or stone-work, for chimneys, hearths, and ovens; so there will be employment for a mason. Can you make bricks and burn lime?

Ed. I will try what I can do, sir.

Mr. B. No man can do more. I engage you. Who is next?

Francis. I am a shoemaker.

Mr. B. Shoes we cannot do well without; but I fear we shall get no leather.

Francis. But I can dress skins, sir.

Mr. B. Can you? Then you are a clever fellow. I will have you, though I give you double wages.

George. I am a tailor, sir.

Mr. B. We must not go naked; so there will be work for the tailor. But you are not above mending, I hope; for we must not mind wearing patched clothes, while we work in the woods.

Geo. I am not, sir.

Mr. B. Then I engage you, too.

Henry. I am a silversmith, sir.

Mr. B. Then, my friend, you cannot go to a worse place than a new colony to set up your trade in.

Hen. But I understand clock and watch making too.

Mr. B. We shall want to know how time goes; but we cannot afford to employ you, at present: you had better stay where you are.

Jasper. I am a barber and hair dresser.

Mr. B. What can we do with you? If you will shave our men's rough beards once a week, and crop their hair once a quarter, and be content to help the carpenter the rest of the time, we will take you. But you will have no ladies to curl, or gentlemen to powder, I assure you.

Lewis. I am a doctor.

Mr. B. Then, sir, you are very welcome; we shall some of us be sick; and we are likely to get cuts, and bruises and broken bones. You will be very useful. We shall take you with pleasure.

Maurice. I am a lawyer, sir.

Mr. B. Sir, your most obedient servant. When we are rich enough to go to law, we will let you know.

Oliver. I am a schoolmaster.

Mr. B. That is a very respectable and useful profession. As soon as our children are old enough we shall be glad of your services. Though we are hard-working men, we do not mean to be ignorant; every one among us must be taught reading and writing Until we have employment for you in teaching, if you will keep our accounts, and, at present, read sermons to us on Sundays, we shall be glad to have you among us. Will you go?

Oliver. With all my heart, sir.

Mr. B Who comes here?

Philip. I am a soldier, sir; will you have me?

Mr. B. We are peaceable people; and I hope we shall not be obliged to fight. We are all soldiers, and must learn to defend ourselves; we shall have no occasion for you, unless you can be a mechanic or a farmer, as well as a soldier. Who next?

Robert. I am a *gentleman*, sir.

Mr. B. A gentleman! And what good can you do us?

Rob. I expect to shoot game enough for my own eating; you can give me a little bread and a few vegetables; and the barber shall be my servant.

Mr. B. Pray, sir, why should we do all this for you?

Rob. Why, sir, that you may have the credit of saying that you have *one gentleman*, at least, in your colony.

Mr. B. Ha! ha! ha! A fine gentleman, truly. Sir, when we desire the honor of your company we will send for you.

Honesty, the Best Policy.

Mr. Day. Well, Mr. Gay, I have been to inquire into the character of your son John, and find that his late employer, Mr. Smooth, thinks he will never do for a merchant.

Mr. Gay. What does he say of him?

Mr. Day. He says that he has no *tact;* by which he means, no dexterity, no skill in driving a bargain.

Mr. Gay. How did he prove it?

Mr. Day. Why, a lady came into the shop, the other day, and bought some silk, and as she was about to take it away, John discovered a flaw in it, and he told her of it; whereupon she, of course, refused to take it, and the bargain was lost; and John was dismissed in consequence.

Mr. Gay. I would not have had him stay, for millions, in a shop where he would have been taught differently. Does Mr. Smooth say that John ought not to have undeceived the lady in regard to the silk?

Mr. Day. He says that purchasers must look out for themselves; and that, if goods are damaged, it is foolishness in the salesman to point it out.

Mr. Gay. Well; do you know what I think of such morality, Mr. Day?

Mr. Day. I should like to have your opinion.

Mr. Gay. Then here it is: I would rather have my son live and die a pauper, than grow rich by such deceit.

Mr. Day. Mr. Gay, I agree with you fully. I wanted to see if the father held to as strict an integrity as the son. Send John to me at once. I will take him into my counting-room, and his salary shall commence this very day.

Mr. Gay. Thank you, sir. I am sure that trickery and deceit are not essential to success in business.

Mr. Day. You are right, Mr. Gay; no man can be said to succeed who has grown rich by cheating. Though he may roll in riches, his life cannot in reason be called a success; it is nothing but a deplorable failure.

Learning and Usefulness.

Thomas   Life is much like a musical instrument on which every one plays to suit himself. Don't you think so, Edward?

Edward. Yes,—and all the better for that. The more music the better I like it. A merry noise always suits me—and any one who don't set his hours to music, has a dull time of it.

Thomas. All this might be very well, friend Edward, if life had no serious duties which call for our attention. Ought we not to improve our minds and get that knowledge which will fit us for usefulness.

Edward. Usefulness! Why, in the present day for a man to prepare himself for usefulness, is like carrying coals to Newcastle. Our country is full of useful men : ten, at least, where one is wanted, and all of them ten times as ready to serve the public as the public is to be served. Why if every man who is qualified should go to Congress, Washington would not hold a quarter of them.

Thomas. You mean all who think themselves fit to go.

Edward. No; I meant as I said.

Thomas. Then what do you think fits a man for Congress?

Edward. Why, he must be flippant and bold.

Thomas What good will that do him if he is without knowledge?

Edward. O! he must have knowledge, to be sure.

Thomas. Well, must he not be a man whom the people can trust? Must he not understand politics, and be willing to serve his country?

Edward. Well, I agree to all that.

Thomas. Then you think our Capitol would hardly hold the men who unite eloquence with confidence, knowledge with honesty, and policy with patriotism? I fear a much smaller space would hold them all.

Edward. Well, I don't go so deep into these matters. But this I know, there are always men enough who want all the offices.

Thomas. Very true. But are there no other ways for doing good, and serving the public?

Edward. Why, yes: one may preach if he will do it for little or nothing; or he may practice law or medicine, if he can get people to employ him; or teach school, if he will live on a trifle and " board round;" but I tell you the country is crowded with *learned* men begging business.

Thomas. So you intend to prepare yourself for the ignorant herd, that you may not be crowded?

Edward. Yes, I have serious thoughts of it. You may do as you please, but I will never ruin a fine pair of eyes in preparing myself for usefulness, —unless the public will give me a bond to employ me when I am ready to serve them. Till such a bond is signed, sealed, and delivered, I shall set my hours to the tune of " Jack's alive."

Thomas. Well, Edward, you have your choice: but I shall set my hours to a more serious tune. I ask no bond of the public. I shall gain all the knowledge I can, that I may be useful and do good in the world—and then when I am called to die I hope to find a rich reward in the reflection that my time has been well spent, and that I have done what I could for the good of others.

The Children's Choice.

JOHN.

I mean to be a soldier,
　With uniform quite new;
I wish they'd let me have a drum,
　And be a captain too:
I would go amid the battle
　With my broadsword in my hand,
And hear the cannon rattle,
　And the music all so grand.

MOTHER.

My son! my son! what if that sword
　Should strike a noble heart,
And bid some loving father
　From his little ones depart!

What comfort would your waving plumes
   And brilliant dress bestow,
When you thought upon the widow's tears
   And her orphan's cry of woe!

WILLIAM.

I mean to be a president,
   And rule each rising state,
And hold my levees once a week
   For all the gay and great:
I'll be a king, except a crown,
   For that they won't allow,
And I'll find out what the tariff is,
   That puzzles me so now.

MOTHER.

My son! my son! the cares of state
   Are thorns upon the breast,
That ever pierce the good man's heart,
   And rob him of his rest.
The great and gay to him appear
   As trifling as the dust,
For he knows how little they are worth—
   How faithless is their trust.

LOUISA.

I mean to be a cottage girl,
   And sit behind a rill,
And morn and eve my pitcher there
   With purest water fill;

And I'll train a lovely woodbine
  Around my cottage door,
And welcome to my winter hearth
  The wandering and the poor.

MOTHER.

Louisa, dear, a humble mind
  'Tis beautiful to see,
And you shall never hear a word
  To check that mind, from me ;
But ah! remember, pride may dwell
  Beneath the woodbine shade ;
And discontent, a sullen guest,
  The cottage hearth invade.

CAROLINE.

I will be gay and courtly,
  And dance away the hours ;
Music, and sport, and joy shall dwell
  Beneath my fairy bowers ;
No heart shall ache with sadness
  Within my laughing hall,
But the note of joy and gladness
  Re-echo to my call.

MOTHER.

Oh, children ! sad it makes my soul
  To hear your playful strain ;
I cannot bear to chill your heart
  With images of pain ;

Yet humbly take what God bestows,
 And like his own fair flowers,
Look up in sunshine with a smile,
 And gently bend in showers.

———•◆•———

What Saith the Fountain?

MARY.

What saith the fountain,
 Hid in the glade,
Where the tall mountain
 Throweth its shade?

SUSAN.

" Deep in my waters reflected serene,
All the soft beauty of heaven is seen ;
Thus let thy bosom, from wild passions
 free,
Ever the mirror of purity be."

MARY.

What saith the streamlet,
 Flowing so bright,
Clear as a beamlet,
 Of silvery light?

SUSAN.

" Morning and evening still floating
 along,
Upward forever ascendeth my song ;

Be thou contented, whate'er may befall,
Cheerful in knowing that God is o'er
    all."

MARY.

What saith the river,
    Majestic in flow,
Moving forever
    Calmly and slow?

SUSAN.

"Over my surface the great vessels glide,
Ocean-ward borne by my strong, heaving
    tide;
Toil on, my brother, life vanisheth fast,
Labor unwearied, rest cometh at last."

MARY.

What saith the ocean,
    Boundless as night,
Ceaseless in motion,
    Resistless in might?

SUSAN.

"Fountain to streamlet, streamlet to
    river,
All in my bosom commingle forever;
Morning to noontide, noontide to night,
Soon will eternity veil thee from sight."

Sunrise and Sunset.

"At evening-time it shall be light."

MARY.

How beautiful is MORNING,
  The childhood of the day;
Fair as an infant's smiling
  Beams its first rosy ray.
How pure and sweet the flowers,
  Its holy dews have kissed;
How gorgeous are its cloudlets
  Of gold and amethyst.
Oh! then, earth, air, and sky, with music ring,
And, like the lark, our souls at heaven's gate sing.
Such be the morning of thy life's young day,
Without a care to dim its rosy ray.

ANNE.

But morn, sweet morn, must vanish;
  The sun ascendeth higher;
The purple clouds are scattered
  Before his glance of fire;
The flowers bend pale and drooping,
  Robbed of their pearly dew;
No lark's glad song is thrilling
  Yon sky of burning blue.
Then comes the heat and burden of the day,
Then must we toil beneath the scorching ray.

Toil bravely on, with patient, willing feet,
For there remaineth yet a rest more sweet.

HANNAH.

Then, lovelier than the morning,
   With soft and rosy ray,
Shall come the peaceful EVENING,
   To crown the well-spent day.
As balmy are the blossoms
   Its holy dews have kissed;
As rich its sunset-glories
   Of gold and amethyst.
Then is the time to rest; 'neath angel wings,
To slumber safe, till a new morning springs.
Thus beauteous be thy life's declining ray,
Thus mayst thou sleep, and wake to endless day.

When We Love the Sunshine.

MARY.

I love the sunshine everywhere,—
   In wood, and field, and glen;
I love it in the busy haunts
   Of town-imprisoned men.

LUCY.

I love it when it streameth in
   The humble cottage door,
And casts the checkered casement shade
   Upon the clean, white floor.

ELLEN.

I love it where the children lie
  Deep in the clovery grass,
To watch among the twining roots,
  The gold green beetle pass.

THOMAS.

I love it on the breezy sea,
  To glance on sail and oar,
While the great waves, like molten glass,
  Come leaping to the shore.

HENRY.

I love it on the mountain-tops,
  Where lies the thawless snow;
And half a kingdom, bathed in light,
  Lies stretching out below.

ALL.

Oh! yes, we love the sunshine!
  Like kindness, or like mirth,
Upon a human countenance,
  Is sunshine on the earth.

Upon the earth,—upon the sea,—
  And through the crystal air
Or piled-up clouds,—the gracious sun
  Is glorious everywhere.

Wishes and Realities.

SUSAN.

I wish I were a little bird
  To fly so far and high,
And sail along the golden clouds,
  And through the azure sky.
I'd be the first to see the sun
  Up from the ocean spring;
And ere it touched the glittering spire,
  His ray should gild my wing.

MOTHER.

Wings cannot soar above the sky,
  As thou *in thought* canst do;
Nor can the veiling clouds confine
  Thy mental eye's keen view.
Not to the sun dost thou chant forth
  Thy simple evening hymn;
Thou praisest Him before whose smile
  The noon-day sun grows dim.

SUSAN.

Above the hills I'd watch him still
  Far down the crimson west;
And sing to him my evening song,
  Ere yet I sought my rest.

And many a land I then should see,
  As hill and plain I crossed,—
Nor fear through all the pathless sky
  That I should e'er be lost.

MOTHER.

But thou mayst learn to trace the sun
  Around the earth and sky,
And see him rising, setting, still,
  Where distant oceans lie.
To other lands the bird may guide
  His pinions through the air;
Ere yet he rests his wings, thou art,
  In thought, before him there.

SUSAN.

I'd fly where, round the olive bough,
  The vine its tendrils weaves;
And shelter from the noon-beams seek
  Among the myrtle leaves.
Now, if I climb our highest hill,
  How little can I see!
Oh! had I but wings, mamma,
  How happy should I be.

MOTHER.

Though strong and free, the *wing* may droop,
  Or bands restrain its flight;
Thought none may stay—more fleet i s course
 . Than swiftest beams of light.

A lovelier clime than birds can find,
　While summers go and come,
Beyond this earth remains for those,
　Whom God doth summon home.

I Can and I Can't.

JOHN.

As through life's journey we go day by day,
There are two whom we meet each turn of the way,
To help or to hinder, to bless or to ban,—
And the names of these two are, "I can't," and "I
　can."

CHARLES.

I can't is a dwarf, a poor, pale, puny imp;
His eyes are half blind, and his walk is a limp;
He stumbles and falls, or lies writhing with fear,
Though danger is distant, and succor is near.

HENRY.

I can is a giant; unbending he stands;
There is strength in his arm, and skill in his hands;
He asks for no favors; he wants but a share
Where labor is honest, and wages are fair.

CHARLES.

I can't is a sluggard, too lazy to work;
From duty he shrinks, every task he will shirk:

No bread on his board, and no meat in his bag ;
His house is a ruin, his coat is a rag.

HENRY.

I can is a worker; he tills the broad fields,
And digs from the earth all the wealth which it
    yields ;
The hum of his spindles begins with the light,
And the fires of his forges are blazing all night.

CHARLES.

I can't is a coward, half fainting with fright;
At the first thought of peril he sinks out of sight;
Slinks and hides till the noise of the battle is past,
Or sells his best friends, and turns traitor at last.

HENRY.

I can is a hero, the first in the field ;
Though others may falter, he never will yield ;
He makes the long marches, he strikes the last blow,
His charge is the whirlwind that scatters the foe.

How grandly and nobly he stands to his trust,
When roused at the call of a cause that is just;
He weds his strong will to the valor of youth,
And writes on his banner the watchword of Truth.

ALL THREE.

Then up and be doing! the day is not long ;
Throw fear to the winds : be patient and strong !

Stand fast in your place, act your part like a man ;
And when duty calls, answer promptly,—*I can* !

What We Love.

MARY.

I love the cheerful summer-time,
　With all its birds and flowers,—
Its shining garments green and smooth,
　Its cool, refreshing showers.

JENNIE.

I love to hear the little birds
　That carol on the trees ;
I love the gentle, murmuring stream,
　I love the evening breeze.

ALICE.

I love the bright and glorious sun,
　That gives us light and heat ;
I love the pearly drops of dew
　That sparkle 'neath my feet.

CHARLES.

I love to hear the hum
　Of honey making bees,
And learn a lesson, hard to learn,
　Of patient industry.

HENRY.

I love to see the playful lambs,
　So innocent and gay;
I love the faithful, watchful dog,
　Who guards them night and day.

SARAH.

I love to think of Him who made
　These pleasant things for me;
Who gave me life, and health, and strength,
　And eyes that I might see.

MARTHA.

I love the peaceful Sabbath day,
　So peaceful, calm and still;
And oh! I love to go to church
　To learn my Maker's will.

Conscience.

WILLIAM.

I have a little voice within
That always tells me when I sin;
I'm sure I know not whence it came,
Pray, sister, tell me what's its name?
There is no one, however near,
Whispers so sternly in my ear;
And often in my lively play,
If any thing I do or say

That's wrong or wicked, then I hear
This gentle tapping in my ear.
I know it is not *Mother's tone*,
Nor Father's, for when they are gone,
It keeps on prompting just the same,
If aught I do *that they would blame.*

MARY.

And, brother, don't it always tell
In kindly notes when you've *done well?*
Are not its whispers always mild
When you have been a duteous child?
God gave not to the *bud nor flower*,
This inward voice of wondrous power.
Ah, no, it only has its birth
In us, who perish not with earth;
Its name is conscience, and 'twill be
A voice from which you cannot flee;
It keeps a registry within,
Rebuking those who live in sin,
And utters words of softest tone
To those who will its dictates own.

Freedom's Jubilee.

BOY.

Father, look up and see that flag,
How gracefully it flies—

Those pretty stripes—they seem to be
  A rainbow in the skies.

FATHER.

It is your country's flag, my son,
  And proudly drinks the light;
O'er ocean's wave, in foreign climes,
  A symbol of our might.

BOY.

Father, what fearful noise is that,
  Like thundering in the clouds?
Why do the people wave their hats
  And rush along in crowds?

FATHER.

It is the voice of cannonry—
  The glad shouts of the free;
This is a day to memory dear—
  'Tis Freedom's Jubilee.

BOY.

I wish that I was now a MAN,
  I'd fire my cannon too;
And cheer as loudly as the rest—.
  But, father, why don't YOU?

FATHER.

I am getting old, and weak—but still
  My heart is big with joy;

I've witnessed many a day like this—
Shout you aloud, my boy.

BOY.

Hurrah! for Freedom's Jubilee!
God bless our native land!
And may I live to hold the boon
Of Freedom in my hand!

FATHER.

Well done, my boy—grow up and love
The land that gave you birth—
A land where freedom loves to dwell—
A paradise on earth.

The Child's Lessons.

MARY.

" Mother, may I stay at home?
I hate to go to school,
And study all the live-long day;
I'd rather be a fool.

" Little birds are flying round,
So merry, bright, and gay;
And bees are buzzing in the vines
The whole long summer day;

" Flowers nod brightly in the wind;
The trees are all in bloom;

And everywhere the sunshine laughs
  But in that old, close room.

"I never want to see a book
  As long as I may live;
And, oh! to play forever,
  There's nothing but I'd give.

"Say, mother, will you give me leave
  To stay out-doors all day;
And with the birds, and bees, and flowers,
  To have my fill of play?"

MOTHER.

"No, dear, you must a lesson learn
  From birds, and flowers, and bees—
From all the sunshine rests upon,
  Green grass and waving trees.

"There's not a creature on the earth
  But has his work to do;
They all obey a Higher Power,
  And so, my child, must you.

"The birds sing praises to our God;
  The bees sweet honey give;
The trees bear fruit, and all the flowers
  Yield fragrance while they live."

MARY.

"But, mamma, butterflies don't work,
  They flit about all day;

· Their little, shiny, gauzy wings
  Are only fit for play.
" And, dear mamma, I'm very sure,
  They'll teach me nothing new ;
And none *seem* happier all the day,
  With not a thing to do."

MOTHER.

" One lesson you may learn, my dear,
  From the giddy butterfly—
It may be 'tis their only work
  To teach it and to die :

" At first they crawl upon the earth,
  A hateful, groveling thing ;
But soon unto a higher life
  They rise, on brilliant wing.

" And you, my darling, too, one day,
  Immortal, shall arise :
Be faithful here, and you shall dwell
  Forever in the skies."

The Echo.

Question.   True faith, producing love to God and
          man,
          Say, Echo, is not this the gospel plan?
          *Echo.** The gospel plan.

---

*From an adjoining room or closet.

Question. Must I my faith and love to Jesus show
By doing good to all, both friend and
foe?

Echo. Both friend and foe.

Question. But if a brother hates and treats me ill,
Must I return him good and love him
still?

Echo. Love him still.

Question. If he my failings watches to reveal,
Must I his faults as carefully conceal?

Echo. As carefully conceal.

Question. But if my name and character he blast,
And cruel malice, too, a long time last;
And, if I sorrow and affliction know,
He loves to add unto my cup of woe;
In this uncommon, this peculiar case,
Sweet Echo, say, must I still love and
bless?

Echo. Still love and bless.

Question. Whatever usage ill I may receive,
Must I be patient still, and still forgive?

Echo. Be patient still, and still forgive.

Question. Why, Echo, how is this? thou'rt sure a
dove!

Thy voice shall teach me nothing else
but love !

Echo.   Nothing else but love.

Question.   Amen, with all my heart then, be it so ;
'Tis all delightful, just, and good, I know ;
And now, to practice, I'll directly go.
Echo.   Directly go.

Question.   Things being so, whoever me reject,
My gracious God me surely will protect.

Echo.   Surely will protect.

Question.   Henceforth I'll roll on Him my ever
care,
And then both friend and foe embrace
in prayer.

Echo.   Embrace in prayer.

Question.   But after all these duties I have done,
Must I, in point of merit, them disown,
And trust for Heaven through Jesus'
blood alone ?

Echo.   Through Jesus' blood alone.

Question.   Echo, enough! Thy counsels to mine ear
Are sweeter than, to flowers, the
dew-drop clear ;

Thy wise, instructive lessons please me
    well;
I'll go and practice them.   Farewell,
    farewell!

Echo. Practice them. Farewell.
    farewell.

What To Be.*

Be patient—life is very brief,
  It passes quickly by;
And if it prove a troubled scene
  Beneath a stormy sky,
It is but like a shaded night
That brings a morn of radiance bright.

Be hopeful—faith will bring
  A living joy to thee
And make thy life a hymn of praise,
  From doubt and murmur free;
Whilst, like the sunbeam, thou wilt bless,
And bring to others happiness.

Be earnest—an immortal soul
  Should be a worker true,
Employ the talents for thy God,
  And ever keep in view
The judgment scene, the great last day,—
When heaven and earth shall pass away.

* By six boys or girls,—one stanza each.

Be holy—let not sin's dark stain
   The spirit's whiteness dim;
Keep close to God amid the world,
   And put thy trust in Him:
So midst thy business and thy rest,
Thou wilt be comforted and blest.

Be prayerful—ask, and thou wilt have
   Strength equal to thy day;
Prayer clasps the hand that guides the world,
   Oh! make it then thy stay;
Ask largely, and thy God will be
A kingly giver unto thee.

Be ready—many fall around,
   Our loved ones disappear,
We know not when our call may come,
   Nor should we wait in fear;
If ready, we can calmly rest;
Living or dying, we are blest.

PART IV.—FOR CONCERT RECITATION.

God is Good.

God is good! each perfumed flower,
　The waving field, the dark green wood;
The insect fluttering for an hour,—
　All things proclaim that God is good.

I hear it in each breath of wind;
　The hills that have for ages stood,
And clouds, with gold and silver lined,
　All still repeat that God is good.

Each streamlet, that for many a year
　Has the same verdant path pursued,
And every bird in accents clear,
　Join in the song that God is good.

The restless sea, with haughty roar,
　Calms each wild wave and billows rude;
Retreats submissive from the shore
　And swells the chorus—" God is good."

The countless host of twinkling stars,
　That sing His praise with light renewed;
(195)

The rising sun each day declares,
  In rays of glory—" God is good."

The moon, that walks in brightness, says
  That God is good! and man, endued
With power to speak his Maker's praise,
  Should still repeat that " God is good."

Hymn of Nature.*

God of the earth's extended plains!
  The dark green fields contented lie:
The mountains rise like holy towers,
  Where man might commune with the sky:
The tall cliff challenges the storm
  That lowers upon the vale below,
Where shaded fountains send their streams,
  With joyous music in their flow. ·

God of the dark and heavy deep!
  The waves lie sleeping on the sands,
Till the fierce trumpet of the storm
  Hath summoned up their thundering bands
Then the white sails are dashed like foam,
  Or hurry, trembling, o'er the seas,
Till, calmed by Thee, the sinking gale
  Serenely breathes—Depart in peace.

*Let this be spoken by a class of six,—a verse each—and let the last verse be spoken by all in concert.

God of the forest's solemn shade!
   The grandeur of the lonely tree,
That wrestles singly with the gale,
   Lifts up admiring eyes to Thee;
But more majestic far they stand,
   When, side by side, their ranks they form
To wave on high their plumes of green,
   And fight their battles with the storm.

God of the light and viewless air!
   Where summer breezes sweetly flow,
Or, gathering in their airy might,
   The fierce and wintry tempests blow;
All,—from the evening's plaintive sigh,
   That hardly lifts the drooping flower,
To the wild whirlwind's midnight cry,—
   Breath forth the language of Thy power.

God of the fair and open sky!
   How gloriously above us springs
The tented dome of heavenly blue,
   Suspended on the rainbow's rings!
Each brilliant star that sparkles through,
   Each gilded cloud that wanders free
In evening's purple radiance, gives
   The beauty of its praise to Thee.

God of the rolling orbs above!
   Thy name is written clearly bright,

In the warm day's unvarying blaze,
  Or evening's golden shower of light.
For every fire that fronts the sun,
  And every spark that walks alone,
Around the utmost verge of heaven,
  Were kindled at Thy burning throne.

God of the world! the hour must come,
  And Nature's self to dust return;
Her crumbling altars must decay;
  Her incense fires shall cease to burn;
But still her grand and lovely scenes
  Have made man's warmest praises flow;
For hearts grow holier as they trace
  The beauty of the world below.

Upward and Onward.

Battling in the cause of truth
With the zeal and strength of youth:
    Upward, raise your banner higher,
Onward, urge your phalanx nigher
    To the centre of the strife,
Strike, where virtue finds a foe—
Strike, while love directs the blow—
    Where the foes of man are rife.

Be your watchword truth and love,
Be your stay the strength above;

'Mid the pure, remain the purest,
'Mid the faithful, be the surest—
     Temperance your banner star.
Ask not rest, nor pray for peace,
'Till the demon foe shall cease
     Life and all its joys to mar.

Warriors in the cause of right,
Earnest in your zeal and might,
Joying in your high endeavor,
Onward press, and falter never,
     'Till the victory be won,
Shout, until the field ye gain,
Press to those which still remain,
     Battling till the work be done.

Little by Little.

One step, and then another,
   And the longest walk is ended;
One stitch, and then another,
   And the largest rent is mended;
One brick upon another,
   And the highest wall is made;
One flake upon another,
   And the deepest snow is laid.

So the little coral workers,
   By their slow but constant motion,

Have built those pretty islands
   In the distant, dark blue ocean ;
And the noblest undertakings
   Man's wisdom hath conceived,
By oft-repeated efforts
   Have been patiently achieved.

Aspirations of Youth.

Higher, higher will we climb,
   Up the mount of glory,
That our names may live through time,
   In our country's story ;
Happy, when her welfare calls,
He who conquers, he who falls.

Deeper, deeper let us toil
   In the mines of knowledge ;
Nature's wealth, and learning's spoil
   Win from school and college ;
Delve we there for richer gems,
Than the stars of diadems.

Onward, onward may we press,
   Through the path of duty ;
Virtue is true happiness,
   Excellence true beauty ;
Minds are of celestial birth,—
Make we then a heaven of earth.

Closer, closer let us knit
    Hearts and hands together,
Where our fireside comforts sit,
    In the wildest weather;
Oh! they wander wide who roam
From the joys of life and home.

Dare and Do.

Dare to think, though others frown;
    Dare in words your thoughts express;
Dare to rise, though oft cast down;
    Dare the wronged and scorned to bless.

Dare from custom to depart;
    Dare the priceless pearl possess;
Dare to·wear it next your heart;
    Dare, when others curse, to bless.

Dare forsake what you deem wrong;
    Dare to walk in wisdom's way;
Dare to give where gifts belong;
    Dare God's precepts to obey.

Do what conscience says is right;
    Do what reason says is best;
Do with all your mind and might;
    Do your duty, and be blest.

Do Good.

We all might do good
 Where we often do ill;
There is always the way,
 If there be but the will.
Though it be but a word
 Kindly breathed or suppressed,
It may guard off some pain,
 Or give peace to some breast.

We may all do good
 In a thousand small ways,—
In forbearing to flatter,
 Yet yielding due praise:
In spurning all rumor,
 Reproving wrong done,
And treating but kindly
 The hearts we have won.

We all may do good,
 Whether lowly or great,
For the deed is not gauged
 By the purse or estate;
If it be but a cup
 Of cold water that's given.
Like the widow's two mites,
 It is something for Heaven.

Sow Seeds of Kindness.

Let us gather up the sunbeams
  Lying all around our path ;
Let us keep the wheat and roses,
  Casting out the thorns and chaff;
Let us find our sweetest comfort
  In the blessings of to-day,
With a patient hand removing
  All the briers from the way.

Strange we never prize the music
  Till the sweet-toned bird is flown !
Strange that we should slight the violets
  Till the lovely flowers are gone !
Strange that summer skies and sunshine
  Never seem one half so fair
As when winter's snowy pinions
  Shake the white down in the air.

If we knew the baby fingers,
  Pressed against the window-pane,
Would be cold and stiff to-morrow—
  Never trouble us again—
Would the bright eyes of our darling
  Catch the frown upon our brow?
Would the print of rosy fingers
  Vex us then as they do now ?

Ah ! those little ice-cold fingers !
  How they point our memories back.
To the hasty words and actions
  Strewn along our backward track !

How those little hands remind us,
  As in snowy grace they lie,
Not to scatter thorns, but roses,
  For our reaping by and by!

Keep to the Right.

"Keep to the right," as the law directs,
  For such is the rule of the road:
Keep to the right, whoever expects
  Securely to carry life's load.

Keep to the right, with God and his word;
  Nor wander, though folly allure;
Keep to the right, nor ever be turned ·
  From what's faithful, and holy, and pure.

Keep to the right, within and without,
  With stranger, and kindred, and friend;
Keep to the right, and you need have no doubt,
  That all will be well in the end.

Keep to the right in whatever you do,
  Nor claim but your own on the way;
Keep to the right, and hold on to the true,
  From the morn to the close of life's day.

Speak No Ill.

Nay, speak no ill! A kindly word
  Can never leave a sting behind,

And oh! to breathe each tale we've heard,
   Is far beneath a noble mind,
Full oft a better seed is sown
   By choosing thus the kinder plan;
For if but little good be known,
   Still let us speak the best we can.

Give me the heart that fain would hide—
   Would fain another's faults efface;
How can it pleasure human pride
   To prove humanity but base?
No; let us reach a higher mood,
   A nobler estimate of man;
Be earnest in the search for good,
   And speak of all the best we can.

Then speak no ill—but lenient be
   To other's failings as your own;
If you're the first a fault to see,
   Be not the first to make it known;
For life is but a passing day,
   No lip may tell how brief its span;
Then oh! the little time we stay,
   Let's speak of all the best we can.

www.ingramcontent.com/pod-product-compliance
Lightning Source LLC
Chambersburg PA
CBHW030829270326
41928CB00007B/963